# true to
# yourself

# THE SOCIAL VENTURE NETWORK SERIES

# true to yourself

## LEADING A VALUES-BASED BUSINESS

*Mark Albion*

## BK

BERRETT-KOEHLER PUBLISHERS, INC.
San Francisco

Berrett-Koehler Publishers, Inc.
235 Montgomery Street, Suite 650
San Francisco, CA 94104-2916
Tel: (415) 288-0260    Fax: (415) 362-2512    www.bkconnection.com

Ordering Information

**Quantity sales.** Special discounts are available on quantity purchases by corporations, associations, and others. For details, contact the "Special Sales Department" at the Berrett-Koehler address above.

**Individual sales.** Berrett-Koehler publications are available through most bookstores. They can also be ordered directly from Berrett-Koehler: Tel: (800) 929-2929; Fax: (802) 864-7626; http://www.bkconnection.com.

**Orders for college textbook/course adoption use.** Please contact Berrett-Koehler: Tel: (800) 929-2929; Fax: (802) 864-7626.

**Orders by U.S. trade bookstores and wholesalers.** Please contact Publishers Group West, 1700 Fourth Street, Berkeley, CA 94710. Tel: (510) 528-1444; Fax (510) 528-3444.

Berrett-Koehler and the BK logo are registered trademarks of Berrett-Koehler Publishers, Inc.

Printed in the United States of America

Berrett-Koehler books are printed on long-lasting acid-free paper. When it is available, we choose paper that has been manufactured by environmentally responsible processes. These may include using trees grown in sustainable forests, incorporating recycled paper, minimizing chlorine in bleaching, or recycling the energy produced at the paper mill.

Library of Congress Cataloging-in-Publication Data
Albion, Mark S., 1951-
    True to yourself : leading a values-based business / Mark Albion.
      p. cm.—(Social venture network series)
    Includes index.
    ISBN-10: 1-57675-378-6  ISBN-13: 978-1-57675-378-1
      1. Small business—Management—Handbooks, manuals, etc.
 2. Social responsibility of business. I. Title. II. Series.
 HD62.7.A44 2006
 658.4'092—dc22                          2005055557

FIRST EDITION
11  10  09  08  07  06     10 9 8 7 6 5 4 3 2 1

Cover design: Leslie Waltzer, Crowfoot Design
Interior design and composition: Beverly Butterfield, Girl of the West Productions
Editing: PeopleSpeak
Indexing: Rachel Rice

*To a foot soldier for transformation,*
*Josh Mailman,*
*who has taught me that the*
*true measure of a leader's success*
*is in the lives touched*

# Contents

# Letter from the Editor of the Social Venture Network Series

Business can be beautiful.

If any overarching theme characterizes the books in this series, that's it. And the notion that starting or running a business can be a joyful experience emerges more clearly than ever in this inspiring book by Mark Albion.

Mark's topic is leadership, one of the most fundamental aspects of any organization—and perhaps the most basic of all. It's no coincidence that academic observers of the world of business have noted a strong correlation between a company's financial performance and its adoption of socially responsible business policies and practices. The explanation they offer? That what distinguishes these companies is *superior leadership*. Their enlightened policies and practices reflect a leader's deeper, more sensitive understanding of the marketplace and the world in which we all live and work. They make a business run better.

Few people anywhere could tackle the theme of leadership in business with more authority or grace than Mark Albion. Mark has approached business from almost every conceivable angle—as an employee, a serial entrepreneur, a consultant, a cofounder and adviser (Net Impact, formerly Students for Responsible Business), a professor (Harvard Business School), and a bestselling author (*Making a Life, Making a Living®: Reclaiming Your Purpose and Passion in Business and in Life*).

Other notable authors have treated the subject of business leadership in general. Some have made extraordinary contributions to our understanding of the topic and how we may internalize the lessons they've learned through painful experience.

But no one previously has addressed the special challenges, and the special rewards, of running a company dedicated to the triple bottom line of people, planet, and profit. That's Mark Albion's turf.

Mark has been one of the leading lights of Social Venture Network for many years. I'm proud to have known and learned from him through all that time. As you make your way through the pages of this book, you'll learn, too. I'm sure of it.

MAL WARWICK
Berkeley, California
May 2006

# Preface

In the fall of 1988, when I was thirty-seven, the first part of my adult work life ended. I left my job at Harvard Business School to build a business that reflected my values. I did have some practical experience. Before I became a professor, I had worked with my father selling real estate.

Dad began his career working with his father in their chemical products company. After many ups and downs, the business failed. So in the summer of 1967, Dad and I went to work for Gulf American Real Estate Corporation, selling undeveloped property in Florida to New Englanders.

Bankrupt and unable to get a bank loan, Dad also sold insurance to pay the bills for his family of six. The following year, he used our real estate commissions to buy options on our own undeveloped property in Florida. We divided the property into several lots and sold them with a ten-year mortgage that we kept ourselves. This meant that we got less money at first (a 10 percent down payment) but a decade of monthly payments with interest, too. We used this cash flow to pay off our cost of the entire property over time while keeping several lots for ourselves.

Through real estate, Dad taught me my first three lessons for building a business:

1. *Nothing is impossible.* You might not have any money, but that doesn't mean you can't start a business or buy million-dollar tracts of land.
2. *Cash is king: keep your costs low and don't take money out of the business.* "Every time we spend one dollar, it

takes ten dollars out of the business," Dad would say. That's because we paid 10 percent of the selling price to secure a property, so, for example, $100,000 would get us $1,000,000 of property (which we sold for a higher price), leveraging every dollar at least ten to one. We still lived frugally for many years after we made good money, not wasting a dollar. All money was reinvested in the business.

3. *Break the rules and do it your way.* Yes, no one who was only sixteen sold land; yes, no one did this business without advertising, dinner receptions, and other marketing expenses that were many times the cost of the land; and yes, no one acted as a bank, keeping the mortgages. But we did. *"Be true to yourself, son. Win or lose, play the game your way."*

The business became very successful. When a worldwide recession hit in 1973–74, the family moved to Florida, while I stayed in New England. Dad decided that it was a good time to slow down the business, stop selling land, and go back to graduate school. I went to Harvard to study business and economics, and Dad went to the University of Miami for graduate work in law. I learned that in business, as in life, there are different stages and that you should heed the rhythms of those stages and act accordingly. ("I thrive on recessions," Dad would say. "That's when you can pick up some great *steals* on property.")

We kept in close touch the next six years through regular visits and daily two-hour phone calls. Dad and I talked about real estate and "the kids," as my two brothers and a sister are over ten years my juniors. They were sent to New England boarding schools and lived with me on the weekends. I even came back home for six months, taking a break from graduate studies to put the business on computer. I assumed that after completing my degrees I'd return to Florida and continue working in real estate with Dad.

But something happened. Something got in the way: *values*. Like Dad, I had to be true to myself. I had to make my own dream come true.

I think Dad always knew. He and I were different, products of two generations, worlds apart. Dad came from the World War II "kill or be killed" mentality of business. He'd always seen business as war, business as survival, and ultimately, business as victory. After all, he spent the nineteenth year of his life in World War II and had his plane shot down twice over Germany. I spent my nineteenth year at Harvard College with no final exams, passing my time at antiwar marches and bake sales, where I'd also meet my Friday-night dates.

Dad knew what his values were. He knew how he wanted to build his business. The question was, did I know my values? And if I did, did I know how to use them to build a business?

I knew that I wanted to make a difference in the community. Whereas Dad might see a development's maximum value as a shopping center, I'd see a good profit in building a gerontology center—desperately needed in the community at the time. But the business could have only one boss, one leader. It was time for me to leave.

I became a professor, though I knew that someday I'd start my own business, just like my father, my mother, both sets of my grandparents, and my uncles and aunts. It was in my blood.

So in the fall of 1988, I took the leap from a world I knew to one that had been invisible to me: the world of values-based small business leaders. I met people who, like me, wanted to use their businesses as a force for social change. People who, like me, had left "good" jobs to build a business their own way, caring about more than a single bottom line. People who, like me, wanted to learn how to combine profit with purpose, margins with mission, and value with values.

All of us learned how to build a business that reflects our values, a business that's true to who we are and who we want to be. These are the values-based small business leaders of Social Venture Network.

Mark Albion
Dover, Massachusetts
May 2006

# Acknowledgments

Thank you, Kathleen Epperson, Marc Gunther, Karen Manz, and Randy Roark for your early-draft reviews.

Without Mal Warwick, board chair of Social Venture Network, there would be no book series.

Without Johanna Vondeling, editorial director at Berrett-Koehler, there would be no book structure.

Without Deborah Nelson, co–executive director of Social Venture Network, there would be no book support.

Without the seventy-five leaders interviewed, there would be no book examples.

And without my family, there would be no book.

# Leading Differently

> Pamela and I talk regularly about the pioneers of values-based business. The members of our network have invented brand-new models, new structures, new forms of leadership, and new ways to serve all stakeholders. But the toughest piece of all is the development of the values-based leader. It's something you learn to become over the course of a lifetime.
>
> DEB NELSON, CO–EXECUTIVE DIRECTOR WITH PAMELA CHALOULT, SOCIAL VENTURE NETWORK

*True to Yourself* is a practical guidebook of strategies, programs, and policies that work for values-based small business leaders. Its intention is to accelerate your learning and help you avoid mistakes to make your job easier, your company more successful, and your life more fulfilling. Its purpose is to make your dreams come true.

But you can't do it alone. The central theme is that, paradoxically, to reach *your* dreams you must help other people reach *their* dreams. Your key task is to design an organization that helps the people you impact do just that—reach their personal dreams—which in turn will lead to your organization's success and the realization of your dreams. At the core of leadership, therefore, is the hard work of building the soft skills necessary to develop and sustain those *relationships*.

## The Challenge of Values-Based Leadership

Being a values-based leader is a *destiny*, not a destination. So why did you decide to become a business leader, much less a values-based leader running a small enterprise where social and financial objectives may conflict daily and one mistake can be fatal?

To illustrate my point, let me offer three potential conflicts:

1. How do you negotiate price with a minority supplier whose business you want to support?
2. How do you lower production costs when it will require that you replace people with machines?
3. How do you maintain an effective, collaborative culture with women in leadership positions when several of the men don't like working for women?

After leaving Harvard in 1988, I faced these three challenges in my start-ups. I could list 100 more. Some I navigated well these past eighteen years; some I did not. The third conflict ruined our culture in one start-up and caused me to sell that company.

I learned that being a values-based leader is not about making one big decision at a critical time. It's about making lots of smaller daily decisions—decisions that may seem incidental but that are actually fundamental to your success. Each can affect many people, strengthening or weakening important relationships. It's also frequently about *how* decisions are made as much as *what* the decision is. It sounds great to say you want every decision to be values based. But try doing it!

Values-based leaders consider the financial, social, environmental, and even spiritual impact of their decisions. So when I use the word "values," I mean standards of behavior for helping people and healing the planet. I mean being concerned with people not only in your company but also beyond your business and immediate self-interest. And I'm pretty stubborn about it. If you can't build a business that leads to a better world for all in some small way, then why build a business at all? The challenge, of course, is how.

Leadership is lonely. Leadership is hard. Values-based leadership is even lonelier and harder. Few may understand your methods or reasoning. When you say you're "values-based," you put yourself under increased scrutiny. You also need more patience, tenacity, and self-confidence to incorporate your values into a financially successful business. In my case, I knew that to do that, I needed help.

## Social Venture Network: Creating a More Just and Sustainable World

When I stumbled upon Social Venture Network (SVN) in 1989, it was like a breath of fresh air. I was introduced to venture philanthropist Josh Mailman, who along with the chair of Calvert Group, Wayne Silby, founded SVN two years earlier. A standing joke in those days was that when anyone was asked, "How did you learn of SVN?" or "How did you get in [to SVN]?" the one-word answer was always "Josh." Josh was everywhere, meeting everyone and supplying the funds and the energy to do whatever needed to be done for SVN to be successful.

Since 1989, we've been meeting at U.S. conferences twice a year and have added regional get-togethers and conferences around the world. SVN has also been the incubator for other successful networks for large businesses, local businesses, MBAs, investors, and inner-city organizations. But our fundamental question remains the same: *How can we as business leaders be a force for social change—while running companies that are financially healthy as well?*

At my first conference, I was like a kid in a candy store with all these incredible people to meet! Still, I felt that I was the only one stupid enough to leave a good job to try to change the world with a small business. To my surprise, I met CEOs, executive directors, and visionary thinkers who had a similar life course.

Though we were doing different types of work, I like to say that we had many heads but one heart.

We shared our business and personal challenges. Some individuals were doing well financially but felt their companies had not contributed enough to society. Others were making a large social contribution but could not get their economics to work.

The SVN get-togethers helped us learn from each other how to marry these worlds of private gain and social good and how to become more personally fulfilled as effective values-based leaders. We also had a shoulder to cry on when things didn't work out. We began what have become long-term relationships—critical to long-term leadership success—within the SVN membership and beyond.

I recognized that our conversations were different from the ones I had during the first part of my career. We were discussing the power of leadership and of business as the power to *serve*. I instinctively knew that these leaders *think, act, and react* differently in dozens of small but significant ways. I felt at home: good-bye loneliness, good-bye problems! Well, not exactly. Remember, you need patience.

### The Process of Leading Differently

With seventeen years as an SVN member, membership in several other values-based fellowships of leaders, and my experience as a values-based leader and writer, I was asked to write a book about this brand of leadership. SVN co–executive director Deb Nelson and I put together a list of eighty-five members to interview. We expected twenty-five responses but received seventy-five. After the deadline, we heard from another five members whom I didn't interview. This 94 percent response tells you a lot about these people and their commitment.

Each interview was conducted over the phone for forty-five minutes with open-ended questions. I then wrote up a 174-page draft of the 75 interviews (66 percent/34 percent profit/non-profit, 60 percent/40 percent male/female, 11 percent leaders of color). The interview draft, my experience, and previous talks with values-based leaders provided the data for this book.

*True to Yourself* is the practical guide to what to do Monday morning at the office that I wish I had back in 1988. It's not a book about the leaders interviewed. Their stories and quotes are used to support and illustrate the advice given. While some of their perspectives on leadership may sound familiar, I want to emphasize how these leaders simply think and act differently regarding the purpose of their businesses. For example, I'll never forget sitting next to Bruce Katz in April 1990 as a new SVN member, Anita Roddick of the UK-based Body Shop, was preparing to address 300 of us. Bruce had recently sold Rockport Shoes to Reebok International, Ltd. He had started the "Walking Movement" and had a positive social impact in many ways. He also had made a fortune. I was thinking, who am I to be sitting next to this guy?

We were hoping Anita wouldn't talk about the Body Shop's products, shampoo and toiletries. We were hoping she wouldn't bore us. She strode on stage with the message that "nobody dreams of selling shampoo all their life. We all dream of noble purposes." She lowered the lights and up came a video.

We were transported to Berlin, Germany. It was November 1989 and the Wall was coming down. Before we could blink, the video moved to Body Shop employees going into Eastern Europe with relief efforts—helping out in orphanages, painting social service buildings. *We could feel their joy.* What an opportunity to serve!

The video ended and the lights came on. Most of us were speechless. Anita had not said one word about her products. She had blown us away instead. Bruce looked at me and asked, "What have I been doing with my life?"

Pioneers like this master campaigner injected a contagious enthusiasm that broadened our perspectives on what a business leader could do. Anita filled us with a positive energy that we'd bring back to our companies after the conference.

The maturity of the values-based business movement—a coming of age, if you will—was reflected in the interviews conducted for this book. While inspired by social activist CEOs like Anita Roddick, many of the movement's leaders have strong business backgrounds. They impose the discipline of business on how they integrate social values into their companies. They are the soul of this book: this "new wave" of values-based small business leaders has taught me how to become true to myself.

[These pioneers] don't set out to change the world; they set out to change *their* worlds. And in so doing, they often change the way one person or a few people or whole communities or entire nations or the world thinks and operates in some significant way.

ANITA RODDICK, THE BODY SHOP

## The Solution: Between These Covers

This book is divided into seven chapters. Chapters 1 and 2 provide a foundation for the five values-based leadership practices discussed in chapters 3 through 7. I conclude with a summary of the key to-dos for a values-based small business leader.

Chapter 1, "The New Values: Transparency, Sustainability, and Responsibility," addresses the strategic requirements of a values-based business leader. Specifically, I replace former General Electric CEO Jack Welch's three levers of business value—reputation, productivity, and regulation—with three new levers that will transform your job.

In chapter 2, "The Three Cs: Competence, Compassion, and Commitment," I argue that these three personal characteristics are essential for every strong values-based leader. All are required to build strong long-term *relationships*—the heart and soul of the work of leadership. I define these character attributes and discuss the importance of developing and modeling them for the entire organization.

Chapters 3 through 7 present the five most important leadership practices I've distilled from personal experience, reinforced by the interviews. The five practices progress from personal leadership to organizational leadership to industry-wide and potentially global leadership: (1) turn your values into value, (2) walk toward the talk, (3) communicate with care, (4) facilitate personal growth, and (5) collaborate for greater impact. Each chapter focuses on specific actions for becoming a more effective values-based leader.

All five chapters are organized similarly. After giving a brief overview of the chapter and its goal, I discuss the importance of a specific practice. Next I offer three myths about that practice, supported by counterexamples based on my experience and that of the interviewees. I then give an example of how to do it effectively and on how not to do it, followed by a set of questions designed to help you improve in the practice. Each chapter concludes with an action exercise so you can practice what you've learned, as well as a summary of the chapter's main points.

Chapter 3, "Turn Your Values into Value," starts with you. It outlines the process of leading from who you are and what you care about to create a "best in class" business.

In chapter 4, "Walk Toward the Talk," I examine what's often the most difficult job: building an internal culture that reflects your values.

"Communicate with Care" is the subject of chapter 5. When you're a values-based leader, everything you say and do—and don't say and don't do—whether you're at work or not, communicates your values to people. I discuss how to increase your sensitivity to what and how you communicate. I use what may seem to be small, but significant, practical reminders to help you maintain the delicate balance of power and responsibility.

Chapter 6, "Facilitate Personal Growth," acknowledges that values-based leaders are agents of transformation, a difficult task that typically faces substantial resistance. I argue that leadership is about changing people's behavior, which is done most effectively by appealing to individual feelings and emotional needs.

In chapter 7, "Collaborate for Greater Impact," I make the case that whereas internal collaboration is important, external collaboration may be even more important to building a business with significant impact. This opportunity, however, requires that you redefine your business and reassess how your time is spent.

I conclude with a review of the major themes in a summary chapter, "Leadership Is Learning."

## Why I Wrote This Book: The Benefit

From my first SVN conference, many small business leaders have inspired me. They've given me hope for a brighter future for my children and your children, a better world for all. But since 9/11, I've come to realize how important our mission is and how there's no better time than right now to develop an army of values-based leaders. In the interviews, Woody Tasch put the opportunity and challenge squarely in front of me.

Woody makes his home on Martha's Vineyard and has a simple lifestyle you might not expect from the chairman and CEO of the Investors' Circle, the largest network of early-stage investors who seek financial, social, and environmental returns on their investments, $100 million to date. His use of solar panels is one of many ways this hard-core venture capitalist is also a hard-core "nurture capitalist." He has his reasons: "Business remains the most powerful force on our planet. Within one or two generations, however, our current form of capitalism will wipe us out. We invest in those passionate leaders who will create companies that care for people and the planet, leaders who will change the direction of the wind of capitalism.

"Growing a small company is a process that can all too easily become about nothing more than maximizing speed and scale. There is an inherent violence in it, a microcosm of the violence the global economy does to communities and bioregions. What we are trying to do is slow down the system with more patient capital, to bring money down to earth, and to create a nonviolent form of capitalism."

Growing a small company is a fast and violent process. Global communication and competition have enhanced that speed and violence. I know we can change that course through values-based leadership. Woody simply helped me realize that to do so I need you on board *now*. Together, we can transform the world.

I've been at this business leadership game for quite a while now and have truly enjoyed the fulfillment of building profitable businesses that reflect my values. I've learned how difficult it is, too. At my core, however, I am a student and teacher; I also helped launch and continue to assist Net Impact (1993), our network for young business professionals. Recently, I've learned more about how to educate values-based leaders from another student and teacher, Gifford Pinchot, known best for his concept of the intrapreneur.

Over 3,000 miles away from the Vineyard, off the coast of Washington State, Bainbridge Island hosts Bainbridge Graduate Institute (BGI), a business school founded in 2002 to change how we train leaders, "changing business for the good." BGI prepares diverse leaders ages twenty-two to sixty-five to build enterprises that are economically successful, socially responsible, and environmentally sustainable. Enrollment is doubling each year, with hundreds now applying for the first MBA in Sustainable Business. How does BGI educate values-based leaders?

"We believe in action learning," professes Gifford. *"Leadership is about building a community of people who trust and support each other.* We help our students integrate the two sides of their personalities—the ruthless business side and the gentle values—and use their gifts here to uphold our motto: 'Leave no one behind. Hold no one back.'"

The students begin each day by meeting in a large circle, talking about what they appreciate about other members of the community. "As a community, we operate in a 'gift economy,' in which we expect nothing in return for what we do for our community, other than respect. We ensure that what each person has to give is made visible to the community and themselves, motivating us all to contribute more. We are teaching not only subjects like marketing and finance but also how to lead."

For example, BGI's computer system was not working well, so four students formed an "action learning team." They interviewed everyone, did their own search on what systems were available, and met with user groups. They persuaded BGI management to buy a particular system and then set it up and trained everyone how to use it.

Gifford muses: "We are cocreating the school with our students in a culture where it is cool to contribute. That experience is essential to their learning how to build a community at work. We give them the opportunity to be recognized and valued, which gives them a strong sense of self. So whereas leadership education is action oriented, its personal impact is highly reflective. Our community mirrors who you are every day—a mirror that develops leaders who make a difference."

*True to Yourself* is my contribution to you. As your business leads to a better world for us all, your success will be your contribution to me.

# The New Values

## TRANSPARENCY, SUSTAINABILITY, AND RESPONSIBILITY

The birth moment for an organization is critical. Almost like conception, the genetics are set, and if you are not conscious of them, they can lead to an organization with a set of values and mission the founder doesn't want. You need to spend a lot of time on your initial mission and values, as they will attract the founding group of people and develop the organization's personality. Be mindful of the founding moment.

MARK A. FINSER, PRESIDENT OF RSF (RUDOLF STEINER FOUNDATION), A $90 MILLION (2005) NONPROFIT FINANCIAL SERVICES ORGANIZATION

In this chapter, we'll learn the three strategic requirements for building a successful values-based small business. The sooner you focus on these organizational values, the easier your job will be. It all starts with your example.

### It's My First Day on the Job: What Should Be My Strategic Focus?

During my years as a Harvard Business School professor, I learned about leadership and strategy from the most successful CEOs of the world's largest corporations. In the 1980s and 1990s, I listened closely to General Electric's Jack Welch, who I believe set the standard for how to lead a profitable global corporation. His leadership mantra was simple: To dominate your markets, you must focus on what will increase your *reputation* and *productivity* or decrease your costs of *regulation*. Your success in managing these three factors will determine the success of your business.

Seasoned business leaders know what their key determinants of financial success are. Many monitor them daily. For a retailer, the key determinant may be shrinkage. If inventory lost from employee theft, shoplifting, vendor fraud, and administrative error is less than 2 percent of revenues, this indicates that the company is running efficiently. For one executive director of a school for challenging teenagers, his barometer is the students' "positive feelings" created at school. He monitors them each night in his office on wall charts of data collected daily.

Whatever these determinants are for your company, CEO Welch maintains that you need to focus on the ones that have the greatest impact on your reputation, productivity, or regulation. Your job as company leader is to ensure that everyone understands that and is working in that one direction.

In small, values-based companies, these three organizational factors are no less important than in more traditional large corporations—at one level. But values-based leaders have broader company goals than CEO Welch and, therefore, a somewhat different set of organizational values as requirements for success.

Many are committed to environmental responsibility. It's not enough to make a simple calculation on what environmental regulations make financial sense to meet. For example, Aveda's founder, Horst Rachelbacher, once told me that when faced with potentially conflicting corporate goals, he expected his people to "report to the Earth." Profitability was important for the personal care products company, but most important was to "care for the world we live in . . . and set an example of environmental leadership and responsibility" (part of the company's mission statement). If there were a conflict between the profitability of a decision and environmental damage, Horst and the culture were clear about what to do.

These values suggest that reputation is built on openness and honesty, what I call "transparency." "Sustainability" denotes longer-term thinking than productivity. "Responsibility" to people and the planet means that you do the right thing proactively instead of reacting to regulation. In this chapter, I illustrate these organizational values with examples of how they impact your job as a values-based leader.

## Leading Transparency: How Much Openness Do You Want?

How much openness and honesty do you want to engage in every day? It's a lot easier to measure your $CO_2$ [carbon dioxide] emissions than the level of honesty and transparency in your company. What it's about is that when you are committed to a certain set of values, like transparency, you will communicate that in all you do, no matter what. Around here, if we mess up, someone immediately tells the person who writes our external corporate responsibility report to make sure that is included.

JEFFREY HOLLENDER, FOUNDER AND CEO OF SEVENTH GENERATION, THE LEADING
U.S. BRAND OF NONTOXIC AND ENVIRONMENTALLY SAFE HOUSEHOLD PRODUCTS

I often think of building a reputation as a marketing effort, an act of persuasion. Transparency builds your reputation as a leader and your business's reputation as a values-based company, too, but in a way that is stronger yet more delicate. Transparency is about being honest, open, and imperfect. Transparency means no secrets (within reason; e.g., trade secrets must be kept)—not only within the company but also in the marketplace. Its cousins are integrity, authenticity, and credibility. Its power comes from its source: *truth*.

## The Power of Doubt and Not Knowing

Transparency requires that you change how you spend your time and how you lead. Listen to Danny Grossman, CEO of Wild Planet Toys, a manufacturer of innovative nonviolent products that appeal to both parents and children and treat girls and boys with equal respect. A former diplomat, Danny speaks thoughtfully and in measured tones: "How do you lead with doubt? How do you express that doubt? It's a critical nuance of leadership. If you don't express it, it will erode your credibility. So I'm clear about what I know and don't know. If we launch a product that I think might fail, I say so and say why, but I also always offer a Plan B, too, in case my doubts prove correct."

Leading with doubt and opening yourself up to other people's opinions and your own imperfections means you should be comfortable with not knowing the answer for everything—and spend time to develop Plan B, too! Women in leadership positions can face even greater challenges.

Nina Simons is the co–executive director of Bioneers/CHI (Collective Heritage Institute), a national nonprofit organization that promotes practical environmental solutions and social strategies for restoring the earth and communities. Though her résumé swells with experience, she has had to overcome insecurities by making peace with *not knowing*: "I've found that *the practice of not knowing has a powerful effect on people.* I had no formal business training, but I did have a strong innate set of skills and talents. I knew that the only way to work toward a leadership position was in an honest way, to recognize repeatedly what I didn't know."

Not knowing allows people to contribute and grow with you. But Nina knows it's important to let others know you don't know in a way that doesn't undermine your authority or sense of self-esteem: "We've all grown up in a culture that tends to value masculine versus feminine traits. There's often an acculturated insecurity among women, a fear of not being up to the task. It's taken me fifteen years to learn to value myself and gracefully accept my not knowing. You need to give yourself permission to fail and communicate that to others. My mantra is 'It's okay to not know.'"

Leadership requires that you continually reinvent yourself. At times you will fail. If you don't, you limit your self-expression and possibilities and create a stiff, conservative culture. Not knowing means that you look at power in a new way.

It's the power of transparency. If you set the tone that transparency is valued in your organization, doubt and not knowing can be celebrated as your leadership credibility rises. The same can be said for organizational transparency.

## The Power of Open-Book Management

Popularized in the 1990s, open-book management calls for financial information to be shared and a process to be developed that enables people to use business information to improve their on-the-job success. It's not only a management tool but also a cultural tool that requires a shared vision and a group compensation system. Some values-based leaders take open-book management even a step further.

Joan Bavaria is the founding president and CEO of Trillium Asset Management, an employee-owned investment adviser. Slight of build but strong in her beliefs, Joan believes that it's essential to have truth in your organization, to have humility and not arrogance: "As a business leader, your job is not a popularity contest. It's to do the right thing and help people become the best they can be.

"Every employee can look at all our financials. All are invited to come in and ask questions after every board meeting. It's so tempting to try to manage what's happening and the dissemination of information. But you must let go of control to have honesty and transparency inside and outside the company. It's the only way to treat your people like grown-ups so that you can develop trust and build leadership in the company. It's the only way we treat anyone involved with Trillium."

For a look at transparency, visit Trillium's Web site and read a full report on the company. You can also read about the company's governance, compensation, and ownership. That's how Trillium builds its reputation.

### Does Transparency Pay?

Like all values, transparency is a process always in need of improvement. Does transparency pay? Here's an example of how the *lack* of transparency hurt one values-based leader:

In the 1980s and 1990s, many values-based small company founders took paternalistic attitudes toward their employees, not treating them as "grown-ups," as Joan would say. They offered great pay and benefit plans. To do so, they took minimal salaries and accumulated little excess capital in the company for a rainy day.

That rainy day came in the late 1990s. For example, one founder who even had full paternity leave benefits for factory workers since the 1970s discovered that his employees were not prepared to accept that profits had been used to fund generous employee benefit programs. They thought that they were being lied to—that the founder had hidden the money somewhere. They couldn't believe how little the founder had taken the past decades for salary. When it was time to agree on some benefit and pay reductions to minimize layoffs, the founder stood alone. He'd never let go of control nor shared company financial information with his employees. He suffered the consequences.

Transparency shifts the burden of leadership. It creates its own culture and requires you to help build the business skills of your employees. It makes information available to others, even to competitors.

Full transparency is not for everyone. It can be personally difficult if you want to keep salaries confidential. (Use salary ranges instead.) It can be professionally harmful if employees leave and take confidential information to a competitor. Hopefully, if you build your organization on the values of trust, honesty, and openness, this won't happen.

## Leading Sustainability: Can You Slow Down Your Business?

I was working in a very healthy ecosystem. Dad made sure every person in his [box] company felt they were a part of a vibrant, collaborative system, not separate from it. He also deeply valued family, vacation, and rest. To stay creative, he knew he needed to rest, and he encouraged others to do the same. His actions set the pace for our ecosystem. His pace told others to slow down, to know when to be the turtle and when to be the hare.

LORI HANAU, PRESIDENT OF GLOBAL ROUNDTABLE LEADERSHIP, SUMMARIZING HER NINE YEARS WORKING AT HER FATHER'S COMPANY

Productivity is often based on working faster, growing more quickly, and reengineering operating systems for short-term efficiencies that may lead to layoffs. Business schools teach young leaders to put together a business plan, get some talent and money, launch the business, establish it, and "flip" it in five to seven years. Lead for the quick money, not a sustainable presence in the marketplace.

Leading a sustainable organization means knowing when to slow down and to take the time to, as Lori Hanau says, "clean up and nourish your own soil. That allows you to access your wisdom and creativity and to replenish what you take out for yourself, for others, and for the planet."

## The Power of Patience

Lori and I frequently discuss our society's cultural obsession with size and speed. You know that if you try to do too much, if you get out of balance in your life, eventually you'll collapse. It's the same with building a company. You get caught up in the hype that bigger and faster is better. It takes you away from building a company that reflects your values and lasts.

I spent the spring of 2005 meeting with retired values-based CEOs of large companies. I asked them what was their primary company goal in their last years as CEO. The similarity of responses surprised me. To paraphrase, "I wanted us to build something special. My first priority was to get everyone to slow down and reflect on what's really important to do to reach our objectives. It's easy to forget in the hectic daily pressures."

Some CEOs instituted daily transcendental meditation. Others used off-site retreats. Several had regular get-togethers to relax and talk about the bigger picture—meetings they attended personally. Many instituted policies that forced people to take time off when it came due. The results were reinvigorated managers, new ideas, and more time spent on what was critical to accomplishing the larger goals. For example, attention to customer needs increased as less time was spent answering intracompany e-mails.

Values-based leaders are stewards, not predators. Make no mistake. Every successful values-based leader I've met has developed a best-in-class company. But it took time. As the president of the investment banking firm Condor Ventures, Adnan Durrani, who's also the founder of Vermont Pure Water Company and an early investor in organic yogurt manufacturer Stonyfield Farm, counsels, "It takes at least ten to fifteen years to build a good business. You need to set a tone that will provide the right foundation. Like Eileen [Fisher] did by slowly building a joyful, egalitarian culture at her clothing company. Or like Gary [Hirshberg] did, taking ten years to build Stonyfield properly—not only to be a sustainable enterprise promoting sustainable agriculture but also one that is cautious about its own use of natural resources and careful about adding external pressures from taking in too much money too soon."

Adnan learned patience the hard way. He had been a go-go guy on Wall Street in the 1980s. He made a lot of money, but "what I was building was not sustainable. I was looking for shortcuts, pushing everyone and myself. I lost myself spiritually. Then, I lost all my money. It was the best thing that ever happened to me. It got me back on track."

The power of *patience* is ultimately the power of *passion*. If you have true passion for building your business, you can wait. You enjoy the journey. At times, that may require you to put a brake on growth.

### The Power of Matching Market Growth to Company Capabilities

Most founders, or at least one of the cofounders, start off as the best salesperson in their company. But as they continue to "do their job," if they are not careful, sales growth can outstrip their people's capacity. This is not easy for them to accept, particularly when they have raised capital and fought hard to increase sales for most of their business years.

A protector of Southern culture, Scott Blackwell is the CEO of Immaculate Baking Company, maker of "cookies with a cause." On May 17, 2003, after nine months of planning, the company made the world's largest cookie. Why? It was a way to slow down what had been rapid company growth and connect with the local community to raise funds for Scott's passion, American folk art. As Scott observes, "We had thirteen people and around $1.5 million in cookie sales. Sales had begun to sky-rocket, but we weren't clearly fulfilling our mission of 'giving back.' I felt like we were straddling a hurdle. I needed to slow down our growth to get our individual capabilities and our infrastructure to fit better. I was causing a lot of stress, so we just stopped taking orders for a while."

Instead, the company strengthened its culture by making a 102-foot-diameter, 38,000-pound cookie—during which time it ran training programs to help employees develop the skills they needed for the next stage of growth. That's how a leader can ensure organizational sustainability.

Few have created a company modeled on sustainability as well as Will Raap. A staunch environmentalist, this Scotsman founded Vermont-based Gardener's Supply in 1983 to sell organic food gardening products. Company sales reached $60 million in 2005, with 250 employees. "We grew the company much slower than our competitors, all of whom are gone now. We knew we had to build not just the business but the capacity to fulfill the business," professes Will.

This concern for organizational capacity first became evident in 1986. Gardener's Supply had grown to thirty people, and Will became concerned that they were losing their sense of community—the essence of a company founded to heal people and the planet through organic gardening. So they adopted a tangible mission internally that would nourish their culture with values consistent with their products and customers. What they adopted is known today as Intervale, "the land between."

Will moved the company's office to 700 acres located a mile from downtown Burlington. It is a historical area of Native American lore, and the eighteenth-century revolutionary Ethan Allen had his farm there. In 1986, however, it was a toxic dump, covered with garbage two to three feet deep. Gardener's Supply developed a nonprofit enterprise to restore it, a cause "bigger than our business, bigger than ourselves, but aligned with our mission," notes Will with pride.

Twenty years later, Intervale is the largest organic community-farming project in America. In 2004, the Intervale Foundation and associated farms produced 20,000 tons of compost and 500,000 pounds of food to serve the local economy. Among the community gardens, bike paths, and nature trails, Gardener's Supply has projects that include marketing its own line of compost products, introducing gardening to at-risk youth, and running a broad-based incubator and training program supporting small organic farmers.

Today, Gardener's Supply is flourishing as it attracts the area's top employees and is the largest purveyor of composting equipment, organic vegetable and flower products, and landscaping and water-saving supplies in the country. Over 25,000 people visit Intervale annually, learning about sustainability and how to implement it in a home environment. The city of Burlington is now a leader in building sustainable communities, in no small part because of Will's vision and creativity, all focused on sustainability—for his people, his company, his community, and his planet.

### Does Sustainability Pay?

How do you know if you're building a sustainable business? Why not ask yourself how you know if you have a sustainable lifestyle? Each question elicits a similar response: you usually know it when you don't have it. Like Adnan Durrani, Katie Paine discovered that if you find out the hard way, the price can be substantial.

Sharp and seasoned, Katie Paine has started several small companies that measure the effectiveness of communication efforts. A 2004 bout with cancer helped teach her about balance in life and business. Her current company, KDPaine & Partners, is built to be sustainable, with personal and professional benefits. Katie did it by avoiding the obsession with size and speed that most leaders have. She offers: "You often need to shrink your company and select clients. It's better for you and for your people. If you keep adding on too many people and too much overhead, you will have to get volume. *Volume for the sake of overhead is lousy.* It will destroy your culture.

"Instead, build a business and a job for yourself that you want to do. Don't accept traditional ways of doing business. Do what you love and make life fun for you and your staff. What makes it fun is having the right number of people on a mission together."

Does it pay? Flying all over the world, exhausting herself to get more sales, CEO Katie had revenue per employee of $80,000 in 1999 with her last company. In her new, relaxed leadership model, revenue per employee has reached $180,000 in a little more than two years!

What's the right size for your company? With all the pressures of running a small business, it's hard to take your foot off the accelerator. Ask first what the right size is for your leadership style and personal needs—the size that allows you inner and outer balance.

It's easy to forget why you started your business in the first place. But as you sign those paychecks each week, you realize that the continued existence of your business is a responsibility you have not just to yourself and your employees but to others as well.

## Leading Responsibility: Is Altruism in Your Best Interest?

Dying would be so much easier than losing my business. It's not because of the money. It's not because of the bruising my ego would take. It's not because my five kids would be completely embarrassed and I'd have to start over and find a new job. It's because if the business goes, I'd be letting down my employees, my customers, my investors, and all the community organizations we support.

LAURY HAMMEL, OWNER-PRESIDENT OF FIVE LONGFELLOW HEALTH CLUBS,
SERVING 12,000 MEMBERS AND DOZENS OF COMMUNITY GROUPS IN 2005

I like to ask business leaders whether their concerns for the broader community beyond their business constituencies is a professional calculation or a proactive personal commitment. For Laury, it's how he breathes. He couldn't do it any other way. That's the difference between leading to avoid regulation and leading to be more responsible.

When I nurture young values-based business leaders, I start by having them answer three questions. Their answers start a personal planning process:

1. What do you see as the biggest social challenge in the world today?
2. What needs to be done to meet that challenge?
3. What roles can you and your company play in meeting that challenge?

### The Power of Social Responsibility

Eight months after the private sale of Kinko's, I saw its founder and former CEO, Paul Orfalea, in Santa Barbara, California. He looked great. The lines on his fifty-five-year-old face were gone, making him look years younger than he did the last time we met. I asked him what happened. He replied, "For twenty-five years, I felt like I had to carry on my back all the family members and friends who invested in me and all our coworkers who invested in our branches [stores]. If I messed up, they'd lose all their money. Now if I mess up, only I lose. What a relief!"

Social responsibility comes in many shapes and sizes, but simply stated, it's about considering interests beyond your own. Paul's sense of responsibility was great, though it was not "outside" his company. The first week we met, he even apologized to me at dinner. He knew what I did and felt bad that he did not do more for those outside Kinko's: "To tell you the truth, Mark, I've been so focused on making sure our coworkers can afford braces and college for their children, I just haven't spent much time thinking beyond them." I told him that what he did for 23,000 coworkers was plenty!

As a values-based leader, your job is to *find your place*. You should choose where you want to make a difference, depending on what values you'd like your business to reflect. In my work, I've tried to help those I could and not hurt others. Each of my businesses has offered different challenges and opportunities. Each has been a vehicle to help society in some ways but not in others. When you run your business properly, you can't separate a commitment to social responsibility from your business. It's the only way you can operate.

When Linda Mason and her husband, Roger Brown, founded Bright Horizons Family Solutions, the largest provider of worksite child care and early education in the world, they did not set their quality standards to meet industry regulations. They *exceeded* them. According to Linda, "We wanted to build a company around great early childhood experience and give our employees the respect and the financial compensation they deserved. To us, profits were our oxygen, and our standards would be the highest possible at that time."

In 1986, the industry was low cost, low quality—just enough to meet regulations. Based on their values, Linda and Roger took a different approach of quality beyond regulations and, therefore, had higher expenses. It would take nearly seven years for the corporate market to see the value of this service.

But from the start, they were clear about what values-based leadership meant to them: "Before we raised capital, we held a retreat to set our mission statement and our organizational values. We told our venture [capital] partners that, while we wanted to provide a good return and exit strategy, our primary responsibility was to our children, their families, and our employees, who needed to be very well trained. The investors bought into our 'social responsibility,' although we didn't have terms like that then."

After a shaky start, Bright Horizons Family Solutions went public in 1997 and had over 600 centers with a capitalization exceeding $1 billion and a price-earnings ratio over 35 in 2005. Over the years, Linda has continued to travel to less-developed regions, such as Dufur in the Sudan in 2005, involving the company in relief efforts. It's all part of a socially responsible strategy set down at the organization's birth.

### The Power of Industry Responsibility

Many values-based leaders take positions in industry associations to advocate important social issues, such as human rights in sourcing from China for the toy industry (Danny Grossman, CEO of Wild Planet Toys) or improving workplace conditions abroad in the clothing business (Eileen Fisher, CEO of Eileen Fisher Company). Though laudable, it's a luxury most can ill afford until their businesses are beyond the survival stage.

Another aspect of industry responsibility can be central to your business and leadership style from the start: your relationship with the other business entities you deal with in your industry. Though these business partners are often considered necessary evils (e.g., brokers, jobbers, distributors) or simply firms to contract from and negotiate with (e.g., manufacturers, suppliers, retailers), values-based leaders find ways to support them.

Soft-spoken and demure, Carol Atwood has a demeanor that can misguide first impressions of this creative, incisive business leader. Her collaborative style has led to much success in the two organizations she's run. For most of the 1980s and 1990s, Carol was president and CEO of TMG (The Merchandising Group, founded in 1947), which provides field marketing services to Fortune 500 companies to help them sell their products and enhance customer loyalty.

Carol agrees that a business leader should have a customer focus, but "in day-to-day practice, you must be focused on the needs of all internal [industry] stakeholders." She provided a rewarding environment for her primarily part-time staff of 5,000, but she also wanted to manage the impact TMG could have on, for example, its Minneapolis-based fulfillment center, as the center's third-largest customer.

"It's not just that if I decided to go elsewhere they would have to lay people off. It's recognizing that if customers beat up on us for speedy fulfillment, it puts pressure on the fulfillment center, which in turn puts the most stress on workers making the clothes in underdeveloped Asian countries. That changes my focus as a leader."

Carol concentrated on how she could reduce the stress of the short time frames so prevalent in the clothing business. For example, if Calvin Klein were coming out with a new jean, it would affect not only production (the suppliers) but also the promotional material that the fulfillment center produces for TMG. How could she help?

"What I did was use our core competence, excellence in market research, to get specific retail reactions early in the fashion cycle and give them to our production and distribution partners so that they could make adjustments earlier in the cycle. A key part of being a values-based leader is *providing a community where every individual counts,* and the boundaries of that community include all your internal stakeholders."

TMG's industry reputation led to numerous national awards for Carol and the company as well as superior results, in large part because of these strong relationships. In 2000, she took the same approach upon founding Spartacus Media, a social mission media company that connects media makers with investors and other supporters.

As you build a business that reflects your values, therefore, think of how you can help make it easier for others to do business with you. I'm not talking about just customers but, as in Carol's case, industry partners, who in turn may find new ways to help you.

### Does Responsibility Pay?

Does being a responsible business leader make a difference? Surveys indicate that it helps you attract and retain the best employees. For example, in my survey of 2,300 MBA students at the top 50 business schools, I found that three-quarters of the students were willing to take 10–20 percent less money to work for a "responsible" company (defined as "a company with values that match yours").

According to a Natural Marketing Institute 2005 report entitled *Corporate Social Responsibility: Consumer Understanding and Influence,* based on four years of annual data from the institute's consumer trends database, 90 percent of the U.S. population says that it's important for companies to be mindful of their impact on the environment and society. Over 70 percent indicate that knowing a company is mindful of its impact on the environment and society makes them more likely to buy its products or services, and nearly 50 percent state it makes them more likely to buy the company's stock. Other surveys show how brand choice is affected even more so by a lack of responsibility.

Let's bring responsibility a little closer to home. The first thought I have as a small business leader is my responsibility to the people giving me their life energy, my employees. I try to hire the right ones, but when things don't work out, it's also my job to let them go. But since firing someone is hugely disruptive to a sense of community, I often have trouble letting people go, or I let them go too late, hurting everyone further.

To begin this section I asked, "Is altruism in your best interest?" If you need to ask someone to leave your company, what higher form of altruism is there than doing it nicely for someone you'll never see again? How you fire that person is an opportunity to signal to everyone the importance placed on valuing and respecting others.

When the CEO of socially conscious Meadowbrook Lane Capital, Joe Sibilia, sold his fountain fruit beverage formulas and technology to the Pepsi Cola Company, he knew that three older managers wouldn't be able to find jobs. So he took $500,000 of his selling price and gave it to them to start a mail-order coffee company with his help and contacts.

Joe's explanation is that "these guys were running the operation, and we figured Pepsi would bring in their own managers. So we gave them a budget to get going on their own." Joe respected the years of great work they'd given him and though he won't admit it, he's the kind of person who feels responsible for people's families, too. By acting like this in all that he does, Joe has bought and sold nineteen companies with lots of support from the most scrupulous investors, former employees, and community groups—all rooting for someone like Joe to succeed.

Alternatively, if you're too slow to fire, that's a problem, too. The national leader in authentic period lighting and restoration hardware, Rejuvenation, was known in Portland, Oregon, for "employees come first but no one else comes in second."

In 1992, founder and CEO Jim Kelly knew the company had a problem. Lots of people wanted to work there, but rumor had it that once you were hired, you were never fired. With about 100 employees at the time, Jim says, "we were becoming fat and stupid. We had to do something about it."

So the company started a cultural correction program for all employees called "Finding the Asshole Within." Rejuvenation went public with it and handled it like a public relations campaign within the company. Designed to ensure that soft hearts didn't get in the way of hard decisions, it was done seriously but made fun. It worked. Fired respectfully, a number of former employees have told others, "That was the best place I ever worked."

## Summary: The Three Leadership Values

This chapter introduced the three fundamental organizational values that should guide your leadership strategy: transparency, sustainability, and responsibility. While related to the traditional strategic levers of company success—reputation, productivity, and regulation—they differ because of values-based leaders' broader social concerns beyond a single financial bottom line.

*Transparency* in leadership requires you to set the example for being open and honest. You'll increase your credibility by being open about what you don't know and also by spending time on alternative plans when you have doubts about an initiative. Company transparency can help employees manage better and take on leadership responsibilities sooner. It also can build business credibility in the marketplace. You should be careful, however, to specify what kinds and amounts of transparency you feel are best for you and the business.

*Sustainability* in leadership means knowing how to pace yourself and your company's growth. At times, it can require you to shrink your company's size to match internal capabilities and to allow you to "select" the best customers. Values-based leaders are patient with company growth and avoid creating a cost structure that demands too much growth, often at the expense of company culture and respect for the environment.

*Responsibility* in leadership begins with a clear understanding of the social value you intend to provide. That value can take many forms, depending on what values you want your business to reflect. Priorities in responsibility to employees, customers, investors, partner organizations, and the community at large should be agreed on and reflected in the company culture. Specifically, how you handle firing people is a powerful symbol of the value of responsibility in your company.

In the next chapter, I present three personal characteristics of successful values-based leaders: competence, compassion, and commitment. Transmitted throughout your organization, these attributes ensure the most successful implementation of transparency, sustainability, and responsibility.

# The Three Cs

## COMPETENCE, COMPASSION, AND COMMITMENT

> Work is a tremendous testing ground of who you are as a human being. Through the practice of Zen [Buddhism], I help business leaders become open-hearted, compassionate human beings. I want them to develop their intellectual competencies, too, but not be blind to the people side of business. The real work of leadership is to keep both sides in the service of other people.
>
> MARC LESSER, FOUNDER AND PRESIDENT OF ZBA ASSOCIATES, A COACHING, CONSULTING, AND FACILITATION COMPANY

Three personal characteristics are essential for every successful values-based small business leader. In this chapter, we'll learn the definitions of these character attributes and the importance of developing and modeling them for the entire organization. They reflect the soft skills necessary for the hard work of building successful relationships—the foundation of the five leadership practices presented in chapters 3 through 7.

## What Qualities Epitomize the Best Values-Based Leaders?

When I joined Social Venture Network in 1989, cofounder Josh Mailman asked me how we could bring the corporate social responsibility movement into the world's business schools. I talked with MBA students and other SVN members, notably social entrepreneur and investor Richard Perl, and after four years of discussions and fund-raising, Students for Responsible Business was born, since renamed Net Impact.

Like SVN, Net Impact is a network—first of MBA students, now of early- through mid-career professionals and graduate students in related fields as well. Net Impact supports these "new leaders for better business" by providing them with an international network and programming to support their careers, education, and volunteer work. In 2005, the international network included chapters in seventeen countries (over 100 chapters in the United States) and 13,000 members.

The Net Impact mission is to help build that army of young, values-based business leaders who will change the way business is done, creating a better world for all. But for me, the question of what they needed to learn remained unanswered for six years.

At the Seventh Annual Net Impact Conference in 1999, "Leadership in Action: Changing the Rules, Changing the Game," the managing director at the time, Daniel O'Connor, raised this challenge in front of 600 MBAs gathered at the University of Michigan: "The true test of our leadership is in how we respond to the overwhelming problems and unprecedented opportunities in the world today. To do so, we will need to clarify our purpose, awaken our passion, and realize our potential—as a new generation of leaders destined to inherit and create the most powerful institution in our society."

I wondered what they needed to develop to clarify their purpose, awaken their passion, and realize their potential as values-based business leaders. In the succeeding years, I learned that the question could be rephrased as, what do they need to develop to be most effective at building healthy relationships? I believe that the qualities of mind and heart, of spirit and will essential to effectively building such relationships come from competence, compassion, and commitment. In this chapter, we'll discuss the importance of these three personal and organizational attributes, illustrating them with leadership examples.

## Competence: All of Us Are Stronger than One of Us

The biggest piece for me as a leader is trying to figure out what we need to know better and once I know what that is, making sure we have the right people to carry it out. I know a lot, but what I don't know could kill us. For example, I figured out early on that I needed someone as passionate about finance as I am about communications. By admitting what I like and am good at and what I don't like and am not good at, I empower us to hire great people and let them do it.

ERIC FRIEDENWALD-FISHMAN, CEO OF THE METROPOLITAN GROUP, A STRATEGIC AND CREATIVE SERVICES FIRM FOR SOCIAL PURPOSE GROUPS

First things first: expertise alone does not make a leader "competent." Moreover, being a competent leader does not mean knowing how to do everything better than everyone else. Not only is that nearly impossible, but as Eric Friedenwald-Fishman says, it's disempowering. If the leader is better than me at what I was hired to do and lets me know it, how motivated do you think I'm going to be?

Being a competent leader also does not mean doing everything yourself. If you do that, what is everybody else supposed to do? While this may sound a little silly, it's a natural tendency for many founders to be insensitive to the need of other people to contribute and feel good about themselves. Founders are used to doing everything themselves and often have trouble depending on others.

Elliot Hoffman led San Francisco's Just Desserts stores and bakery and 250 employees successfully for over twenty-five years, but he finally lost the company. His assessment: "I was out of balance. I was inspired to build an organization that respected people and connected us with the community, but I didn't spend enough time focused on the real nitty-gritty of the business. I felt that if you're really going to be an inspirational leader, you can do that and manage everyday operations, too—'a real man can do it all.' I realized I should have brought in someone who was equally passionate about operations."

Competent leaders know how and when to let go of control. They unleash the potential of others, motivating them to find their own greatness. In so doing, they create an organization of committed members, each recognized for his or her contribution.

Many of the most competent leaders I've known have had learning disabilities. Dealing with conditions that often went undiagnosed until they were teenagers, they found school difficult. That caused self-esteem problems but also gave them a respect for the abilities of others. One such leader told me, "When I started my company, I was so happy smart people would work for me that I gave them freedom to do things their own way." These CEOs are revered for their talents and for how they build communities of talented people allowed to use their gifts.

Of course, you don't need disabilities to recognize the abilities of others, to know how to create work that uses their strengths. Yet many competent leaders tell me that the most important thing they do is "hire people who are smarter, who are better at things than I am, and who really buy into our mission and values." I believe that personal and organizational success is based on this relationship-building skill more than any other.

---

MY DEFINITION OF
**COMPETENCE**

A competent values-based leader translates the mission and values of the organization into practice, creating a values-based context for all decision making.

---

Of course, you need to be sharp, do your homework, and work hard. It's your job to stay on top of the situation. When you're values based, when your style of leadership isn't the norm, attention to detail is even more important for building trust and confidence.

So is leadership competence that simple? Know what you know and hire people who know the rest, while creating the proper context for growth and expression? Not quite. To know when to step in and make hard decisions, a competent values-based leader must set clear boundaries, as personal values and the public marketplace can make strange bedfellows.

### The Importance of Boundaries for Values

It's important that your values don't lead to unnecessary business mistakes.

Seth Goldman, president and "Tea-EO" of Honest Tea, the national leader in organic bottled beverages, learned the hard way. He launched what he thought was a great tea, Haarlem Honeybush. Honeybush is a rare indigenous herb the company purchased from Haarlem, a subsistence farming community in the Western Cape province of South Africa. Seth shared a portion of Honest Tea's revenue with the farmers to help them expand, which meant more tea could be produced for the local or international market. But "our values blinded me from seeing that this was not a market-based product. It had ingredients unknown to the consumer and a taste profile they weren't used to. It was unsweetened, and the label was unusual. These were too many steps for our consumer to take, and it flopped," admits the thirty-seven-year-old straight-talking leader.

A few years later, Seth introduced the first fair-trade-certified bottled iced tea, Peach Oo-la-long, with great success. It had a great taste profile, which meant people understood what they were getting—peach and organic oolong. The label designed used a comic strip familiar to the customer, *Bloom County*. And the company added a little bit of organic sweetening, which is more customary in bottled beverages. Seth's analysis: "Our products need to be accessible. While I need to make sure that we stay true to our values, and I will continue to listen to my heart, I also have to make sure my values don't take us too far away from the marketplace. For example, we're now bottling not just with glass but also with plastic, which can be environmentally conscious, too. That packaging allows us to get into chains like Target [discount stores]. My job will be to make sure we educate our customers on the ecology—the why and how we are packaging with plastic."

Seth recognizes that translating values into practice can be complex and that many factors should be taken into account before decisions are made. It means that he knows what he's willing to do and not do in terms of negotiating the values behind how and what Honest Tea produces.

### Negotiating Boundaries for Values

Seasoned serial entrepreneur Florence Sender is the CEO of a natural bath and body products company, FoodLogic. Florence is a change agent with a social agenda that promotes responsible, sustainable business practices. As a competent leader, however, she, like Seth, is clear about her standards. In her words, "Those standards are the fabric of my business. For example, the market wants color on the shelf, so we make colored bottles instead of coloring our products. We have standards for the work environments of our suppliers. And we have other rules, too, that are part of our 'Ten Commandments.' To keep them and negotiate well requires that I have an exceptional amount of industry knowledge and clarity about our boundaries in how we do business. So I need excellent staff to keep me fresh and advise me."

Florence is clear that FoodLogic is a business and must do business to survive. Though she never violates her values, she acknowledges market realities. For example, when she chooses a supplier, she will select an employee-owned or a minority-owned company over others, but she does not insist that FoodLogic does business only with those companies because "I still have to produce the right product at the right price and make money."

To see boundary negotiation expertly put into action, let's go behind the scenes to one of Florence's recent negotiations.

Like Seth, Florence recently approached Target about carrying a new product: stress-relieving bath salts called "Bath Rocks." A woman-run factory produces the salts, an employee-owned company creates the unique packaging, and a facility that employs handicapped people puts them together by hand. The shipping boxes come from a family business, and Florence uses small neighborhood truckers. All are U.S. companies.

The Target buyers told Florence that they have their own approved list of truckers. They also wanted a lower price than she needed to cover her expenses. They informed her that she could lower her costs by having the product made in China. She refused. A deal breaker? Not when your staff has prepared you like Florence's had!

Florence was able to tell the Target buyers exactly what everyone else was doing in the industry. She described her suppliers, asking the buyers, "Do you want to put these people out of business over a few cents?" It was the first time they had even thought of the possibility of doing business differently. She agreed to consider using their truckers. They decided to take the products without further price or cost discussion. The deal was done.

What's negotiable and what isn't? You must know the boundaries where your values meet the marketplace. By the way, after that meeting with Target buyers, Florence went to JCPenney, gave the buyer her list of suppliers before they began to talk, and was asked by the buyer if anyone on the list was from China. When Florence said no, the buyer responded without even looking up, "That's good," and took the product.

Competent values-based leaders know where their boundaries lie. They negotiate but don't retreat from the edge of their values. They educate one person, one company at a time, building trust and relationships. They listen and assess, for even though people care about how much you know, they care even more about how much you care about them.

## Compassion: Selfishly Seeing Yourself in Others

We spend a few weeks each year consuming the product we produce. We live in the same apartments as our clients, take the same hikes, and meet with as many clients as we can when we are in Europe. Customers respond that they feel like insiders, like part of a movement or family, not like clients of a company.

OCTOGENARIAN HAL TAUSSIG, FOUNDER AND CEO OF IDYLL LTD. AND ITS EUROPEAN VACATION RENTALS SUBSIDIARY, UNTOURS, RECIPIENT OF THE 1999 MOST GENEROUS COMPANY AWARD FROM PAUL NEWMAN AND JOHN KENNEDY

Do you feel the joy of others as your joy? Do you bear the grief of others as your grief? Compassion may start with how you treat employees, but for values-based leaders it extends to how you treat *everyone* and includes the health of your very business, as Carol Atwood showed (chapter 1) by minimizing the stress put on distributors in busy times.

Consider the reasons SVN cofounder Josh Mailman believes that an emerging public issue is the importance of buying and supporting the production of organic food and cotton. Healthier food and a healthier environment are two reasons. But this issue is also essential for the millions of small farmers in the developing world if they are to live without being poisoned by pesticides that they currently use for nonorganic products without the means or knowledge to protect themselves. As world opinion becomes more sensitive to these issues, keeping workers healthy and happy isn't just compassionate. It's also good business.

Compassion is the quality of empathy that leads to a healthy respect for others and a sense of accountability. A cousin of responsibility, compassion often leads to what society calls more responsible actions. However, if compassion is to be sustainable, it must work in the best interests of you and your company, too.

It's important to be clear on what compassion is not. Often, in the interests of being compassionate, values-based small business leaders go too far, overlooking what's really best for all concerned. For example, if you're too generous with your staff, you may undermine the sustainability of the company and their jobs.

Even more dangerous is how values-based leaders react to the need for downsizing when business slows. Often, they are too slow to let people go, disrupting the company's community and viability more than is necessary. During the recession of the 1990s, I heard the same story repeatedly. To paraphrase, "I held on to people as long as I could. Then I realized I just had to let some go. So I let go the least valuable first but felt so guilty that I gave them great severance packages. Soon I found out I had let go far too few people. By the third round of layoffs, I was letting go some of our best people, but by then I couldn't even give them a minimal severance package."

Waiting too long, being too generous at first, and laying off too few people at a time compounded these leaders' problems. That's why competence and compassion are tied so closely together. One of your biggest responsibilities is to keep people employed in fulfilling, well-paying jobs. Better yet, many values-based leaders are creating more democratic cultures. Employees vote on what to do. Facing layoffs, they often choose to save jobs by reducing their work hours and compensation until business picks up.

---

### MY DEFINITION OF
### COMPASSION

A compassionate values-based leader respects the individual needs of all who are impacted by the organization, acting in the best interests of all.

---

Of course, compassion is about caring for others and, at times, putting their needs before yours. But values-based leaders go one step further—they try to transform a capitalist system that leaves many in its wake into one where everyone is considered and all can win. That is, they try to replace the invisible hand of competition with the visible hand of compassion. Those are big goals accomplished primarily through many small, incidental acts of leadership that make a fundamental difference in how you do business.

As a small business leader, you are likely to underestimate your effect on others—the symbolism of your every act. And when you're values based, the scrutiny is even greater. Everything you do and say carries greater weight and importance than if it came from anyone else. Your opportunity to promote compassion, therefore, is determined by your perceived authenticity and by your respect for the needs of running a business.

## Treating People as Equals

It's important that you model what compassion is and understand what it is not.

Gun Denhart carries herself as someone who doesn't want to intrude. A natural, lithe woman who's comfortable with herself, Gun's presence draws respect through her quiet self-confidence and interest in others. Cofounder of $100 million children's clothing company Hanna Andersson, CEO Gun led finance for nearly twenty years, but she also exemplifies the soft skills. She's the epitome of the values-based leader who respects her followers. Compassion may be most evident in her employees' community involvement, yet Gun models it in many routine daily activities.

For example, Gun believes it is important to be respectful of all people's time. At Hanna, meetings start on time since "I don't want to penalize those who show up on time. I think this practice leads to respect for others in many ways throughout the company." Another example is on display when Gun walks into an office where coworkers are talking, trying to solve a business issue. What does she do? "I wait and let them continue talking until they've finished. If it goes on for a few minutes, I'll leave and come back. But I don't break in, interrupting their work. Unfortunately, I've seen that rudeness many times when 'important people' come into a room."

Gun also has learned what compassion does not mean: "When we started Hanna, I did a lot of listening, perhaps because I am a foreigner [Swedish] and not familiar with the American way. I thought we could operate as a democracy, all peers. Up to fifty people, I thought we should all sit together and make decisions by consensus. I was so naïve. I soon learned that there would be times when we would not agree and that I then had to be the one to make the final decision."

Also partially due to her European heritage, Gun always saw Hanna as a lifelong family. She thought that when people came to work at Hanna, they'd stay forever. If someone left, she felt the company had failed in some way. But she learned that if Hanna was truly a compassionate company, "our job was to help [employees] learn and grow on the job and to respect their need for a balanced life. If at some point they decided to leave the company, we could feel good that they had learned new skills and hadn't sacrificed their families for their jobs. Other times, if we had to let them go, we felt it was best for all concerned."

Gun and her husband, Tom, the head of design, sold Hanna a few years back. Gun now leads Hanna's children's foundation in the Portland, Oregon, area, working elsewhere as well to advance children's welfare.

She has learned that compassion in action must be tempered by the realities of running a business—any business. How that's done depends on your leadership style.

### Loving and Being Loyal

The relationship between compassion and loyalty is delicate, with no one right way to balance the two. Laury Hammel operates differently than Gun Denhart does but with similar values that respect people and relationships.

As unassuming as Gun appears when you first meet her, the opposite is the case when you meet the owner and president of the five Longfellow health clubs. Laury is a ball of energy, a force field of passion and compassion that he wears on the sleeves of his ever-present athletic clothing outfit.

Laury takes it personally if *anyone* decides to leave his company. He still uses the same architect, the same insurance salesman, and just about all the same vendors as he did twenty years ago. When offered a lower price by another vendor, he gives his vendor a chance to come within 10 percent of that price to keep the business. All his vendors have been able to do it so far. "Hey, our vendors have to make a living, too," asserts Laury. "And by keeping these relationships, it allows us to spend our time on more creative ways to serve our customers."

Longfellow health clubs are known around town as the "love clubs." Their motto: "Loving our customer. Loving our staff." How does this actually happen? "We can't even get mad at you. You're so nice!" exclaimed a couple. They had come for a swimming lesson, after which they were flailing around in the lap lane at a time when it was bothering serious swimmers. The lifeguard suggested another time nicely, but they were upset. They stormed their way to the front desk.

"Our front desk person for over twenty years, Sandie, knew the couple had joined that day," explains Laury. "When they got to Sandie, she walked around the desk to them and said, 'I think you need a big hug. We're sorry.' That's why they couldn't stay mad at us."

That same philosophy translates into how Laury treats his managers and employees. He admits that he has kept people on too long: "Sometimes we don't fire soon enough or at least ask some tough questions of certain employees early enough." At times this has caused havoc. In one instance, Laury knew a manager was having a tough time but overlooked it. When a number of good staff members left because, as he was told, his loyalty to his managers got in the way of his staff, he took care of the situation. He met personally with the manager, explained clearly what he was told and why he was letting the manager go, listened at length to the manager's explanation, and then let him go on good terms.

Laury also adjusts to the needs of individual staff members. A few years ago, he hired a personable tennis instructor whom my club had just let go because of his inability to show up consistently. He's a hemophiliac. Laury made it clear that he should do what he felt he could and not worry about it.

People notice those kinds of things. And compassion spills over to other staff behavior. In the past, when Laury has had financial troubles at the clubs, the first people to offer him money *unsolicited* have been his staff. The second group has been his loyal customers.

Compassionate values-based leaders model daily in many small ways how they care for others and are sensitive to what's required to build strong relationships and maintain a healthy business. To maintain that balance through the ups and downs of running a company takes a lot of determination, will, and commitment.

## Commitment: It's Not about the Money

Candle Cafe is not a business but a lifestyle choice for us, our staff, and our customers. We've had a lot of employees and customers with us eight to fifteen years now and have changed their lives and ours through learning about food and health. We bring organic fresh food from the farm to your table, and as we use no animal products, our business is committed to nonviolence.

BART POTENZA, CO-OWNER WITH JOY PIERSON OF TWO NEW YORK CITY
VEGAN RESTAURANTS

In 2005, Bart Potenza was sixty-seven years old and proud of the fact that he hadn't been sick once in the past thirty years. For Bart and co-owner Joy, Candle Cafes, the first "green" restaurants in New York City with extensive in-house environmental programs, are an expression of who they are and how they live. It's how they touch the world. They're as committed to those cafes as they are to themselves and each other.

People can *smell* commitment in a leader. They know why you're here and why you're doing what you're doing. And your commitment inspires commitment from them. So what is this quality of commitment? What is this quality that most of the Fortune 500 CEOs I've talked with desire more in their workforce than any other?

Commitment is easy when you're starting out. Salaries are low or nonexistent and company stock has little value. Hopes and dreams are your daily bread. Of course, you attract people committed to the social need that your business addresses. Why else would you and they be there? This is a valuable advantage for small business leaders.

Commitment is commonly believed to be tested when business doesn't go well. That's true, but in my experience the real test is when you have financial success. Employees join with good starting salaries. Company stock has value. You may receive that first offer "you can't refuse" for the company or your services. What should you do?

Take a moment. Why should you be concerned when you're just starting out? If you take in outside capital, you do need an exit strategy so investors know how they'll get their money back. If business doesn't go well, you try to make it work. But if your company is a success, the question is, have you built it in a way that lets you do what you want to do?

The sell/don't sell issue—the legacy issue—dominates discussions of what it means to be a committed leader in many small business circles. SVN members have built sizeable companies, and some have sold them to Fortune 500 companies. A few had lost control of their companies and had no choice. Others say they sold to have a larger social impact through the increased resources and customer bases they can now access.

The "don't sell" contingent argues that if you're committed, you can't sell your company to some anonymous large entity that you know will never be as committed as you are to the same cause and values. Similarly, if you take your company public, not only do you lose control but also few founders stay on for more than a year or two. The argument is, therefore, that if you're truly committed, you'll maintain control of your company no matter what and will do what's necessary to support that decision right from the start.

Danny Grossman launched Wild Planet Toys in 1993 to provide positive experiences for boys and girls without relying on violence. After ten years of significant revenue growth, he thought seriously about selling the company. After all, didn't he learn at business school that you build a company, flip it, and then move on? He recalls: "We were going through the dot-com boom, and it could be distracting and demoralizing to run a real business in that environment. But when I realized that my two sons were the age of our target market, I fell in love with the company all over again." Taking a leadership role in the industry, Danny is now recommitted to building a better world for sons Noah and Jonah and to taking the company to new heights.

In 2000, Gary Erickson and his wife, Kit Crawford, faced the sale of Clif Bar, the $100 million maker of energy bars. They decided not to sell and bought out their partner, and Gary took back the CEO reins for four years. In 2004, he turned over the job to Sheryl O'Loughlin, who had been groomed for the job for several years. Gary counsels: "Leaders don't let go soon enough. They wait too long, can't find someone, and have trouble delegating. The company loses momentum; you burn out and sell out. Sheryl allowed me to recommit to the company." Gary is now involved in the "aspects of the company I love, like new product development," keeping him as committed as ever to Clif Bar.

Commitment may seem easier in a cause-driven, not-for-profit organization, yet many such companies suffer from inadequate funding and employee burnout. For-profit businesses may be mission driven, but the demands of the financial markets

> ### MY DEFINITION OF
> ### COMMITMENT
>
> A committed values-based leader brings his or her deepest desires and most profound dreams into the core of the organization and its community in a form that's vibrant, meaningful, and inspirational for all stakeholders.

can end up directing the daily work. That's why your role—how *you* are committed—is as essential as the cause itself.

A few years ago, the CEO of a multinational asked me to fly to Europe to find out why his company's sales had plunged. I engaged the twelve division presidents in all-day and all-night sessions. At four in the morning, the president of the largest division, an eighteen-year veteran and the 11,000-person company's second ranking woman, who rarely spoke at these meetings, admitted, "I don't believe any more for the first time in my career. And if I don't believe, how can my people believe?"

You should believe that your work at your company is the best way to achieve your personal mission. But few companies will last your lifetime, and over time, as you and your company grow, more effective ways may emerge for you to make a difference. Commitment is not about the company or its form. Commitment is about being true to the mission that attracted people to your company in the first place—starting with you.

### Commitment as If the World Is at Stake

Depth and clarity of commitment help you motivate others to be as committed as you are. When people hear your name, can they say immediately what you stand for?

If you didn't know that she could be a salsa dance champion, you'd think Amy Domini is all business. In many ways, this bright, iron-willed leader is just that. Commitment personified, Amy's mantra is clear: *"Remove the barriers to socially responsible investment.* If we do that, it will allow us to tell a story of a more just and sustainable planet for our children to grow up in. I don't think there's any other force strong enough to stand up against finance."

Back in 1981, Amy researched the phrase "corporate social responsibility." Three weeks later she received one relevant article. For years, Amy believed that the world was at stake and she was the only one who knew it. She confesses, "That's why I was so desperate to hang on until we made this happen."

In 1988, Amy cofounded KLD Research to promote the importance of a company's social responsibility record. On May 1, 1990, she launched the Domini 400 Social Index, a common stock index like Standard & Poor's 500 Index (the S&P 500). The two indices share 250 companies. The 150 companies that complete the Domini 400 Social Index provide industry representation of companies with particularly strong social characteristics. The index has outperformed the S&P 500 over the past fifteen years, thus demonstrating the importance of social screening in valuing corporations.

Commitment? Amy went eleven years without a salary. She reached her limit on her credit cards and rented out rooms in her house. She held on to her day job as a trustee with Loring, Wolcott & Coolidge, advising socially responsible investors. What did she accomplish? Amy is pleased to tell you: "No one knew what a sweatshop was. Today, we get a 'friendly' company, the Gap, to be a 'fair labor' poster child, and then Nike and others follow by listing all their contract factories. Today, Procter & Gamble becomes the largest producer of fair-trade coffee. Today, Fortune 500 CEOs call and ask how they can do a corporate sustainability report. Today, over 2,000 companies have corporate sustainability reports. It's now an established field."

If you know Amy, you know what she stands for. Known affectionately as the "godmother of the social investing movement," she translates her commitment into nurturing her staff of thirty, educating them to grow on the job so that they can become as committed as she is. She sends at least six people each year to the Socially Responsible Investing conferences in the Rockies, sends people in rotation to take relevant courses, and introduces her staff whenever possible to leaders in the field.

Amy has joined the select few named by *Time* magazine in 2005 as one of the most influential people in the world and was the only one selected from the world of finance. During recent years, she has used her fame outside her company, serving her mission through speeches, writings, and considerable travel to develop more converts committed to people and the planet through capital.

### Finding the Best Form for Your Commitment

Many of our most financially successful SVN members would laugh at the mention of money when they think back to how they started their companies. To paraphrase, "It was always about making a contribution, doing something for others without much of a sense of how we were going to make money doing it. We hoped that would work itself out."

Commitment often leads to financial success, but if you don't have that commitment, it's much more difficult even to get started. When I owned my Vermont-based environmentally responsible dog biscuit company, my partner and I had a chance to grow the company substantially, but he didn't want to do it. Given the excellent financial outlook, I thought I'd do it alone. I went to a venture-capitalist friend who had told me years before that he'd back any business I'd work at 100 percent of my time.

I explained the business and my 100 percent time commitment. When I finished, he turned me down cold: "I wouldn't give you a cent. You sound like a brainy MBA. I don't feel any heart, any real commitment to what the company is trying to do." He was right. I was building the business primarily for my partner, who was a dog lover. I had no real interest in the product. I saw the excitement of the financials, not of the mission.

That's not what it's like for Jane Hileman, founder and CEO of the American Reading Company (ARC), home of the 100 Book Challenge, a systemic independent reading program to help every child in America read at or above grade level. Commitment is apparent at every level of the program, from CEO to consumer.

Jane was a schoolteacher for twenty-eight years and for twenty-eight years was frustrated with the huge achievement gap between rich and poor students. She believed that this was largely the result of a difference in their reading habits from birth. She reflects: "All I thought about was how to get the kids to read. The average reading level in our urban high schools is third- or fourth-grade level, and that's of the 50 percent who have actually stayed in school. I was determined to figure out a way to change this unnecessary situation, whether through a nonprofit or for-profit I wasn't sure."

The best form for Jane's commitment turned out to be a corporation. Jane grew the company around her mission as "it's never been about the money. Many of us are lifelong educators who have spent our careers working in the inner cities. We're 100 percent committed to getting the kids to read, and every investor knows that's what we're about." In the first three years, Jane grew ARC into a $5 million company without any financing other than what came through customer orders.

In eight years, ARC has grown to $13 million in sales and 100 employees in 2005, with the 100 Book Challenge program implemented in 650 schools and 26 states. Jane likes to hire family and friends. She acknowledges that others consider this a mistake, "but I know them and know they're as committed as I am. The community feeling is important to me." To demonstrate the clarity of their commitment, all Jane's employees are asked to write a business plan and connect what they plan to do at ARC with what they want to achieve in life.

ARC's mission is to get students committed, too. "Children have to be agents of their own lives," notes Jane. The students choose what level and type of book to read. They must read at home and at school, and their reading is tracked with log sheets like a Weight Watchers program. They earn prizes and medals for who is the most committed, who is working the hardest, not for who is the smartest. ARC also teaches the teachers how to support the students.

In January 2005, Random House became a minority shareholder in ARC. Jane maintains full operational control with written agreement to a triple bottom line that includes her commitment to high quality and social responsibility along with profitability. But she also wants to grow and get to scale, as "we're committed to the type of paradigm change that should sweep the country." Now that's something worthy of commitment.

### Summary: The Three Leadership Attributes

This chapter introduced the three personal characteristics that are the foundation of successful values-based leadership practices: competence, compassion, and commitment. They combine the traditional requirements of excellence with a leadership style that goes beyond immediate financial returns and personal success. They allow you to clarify purpose, awaken passion, and realize people's potential through mutually beneficial business relationships.

*Competence* in leadership is not about knowing how to do everything better than everyone else or doing everything yourself. Competent values-based leaders translate the mission and values of the organization into practice, creating a values-based context for all decision making. They help people reach their potential and are aware of the daily requirements for business success. They know how and when to let go of control, hiring people who complement their abilities and passions. They recognize the boundaries between their values and market requirements. They know how to manage that delicate balance, not letting values blind them from perceiving customer needs clearly.

*Compassion* in leadership is the quality of empathy that leads to a healthy respect for and a sense of accountability to others tempered by business needs. Compassionate values-based leaders respect the individual needs of all who are impacted by the organization, acting in the best interests of all. They don't mistake compassion with being overly generous with staff or with being too slow to fire people when necessary. They're comfortable making hard decisions with tough love.

*Commitment* in leadership begins with a clear communication of the purpose of the organization and the long-term plans for the business and its founder. Committed values-based leaders bring their deepest desires and most profound dreams into the core of the organization and its community in a form that is vibrant, meaningful, and inspirational for all stakeholders. That depth and clarity of commitment allows them to attract and motivate others to be just as committed. While the form of commitment may change, the mission remains.

In the next chapter, I present the first of five practices of successful values-based leaders: turning values into value. As in all of the practices, successful leadership comes from your ability to infuse your organization with competence, compassion, and commitment—your skills in building relationships that help you realize your dreams as you help others do the same for themselves.

# Turn Your Values into Value

Everyone is always trying to find out, How can my business be different from someone else's? How can my business be unusual? Well, don't look too far, because the way that your business can be unusual is by having it reflect yourself. Everybody is different, and if your business actually reflects you as an individual, it's going to be different. My business expresses who I am.

JUDY WICKS, FOUNDER AND CEO OF PHILADELPHIA'S WHITE DOG CAFE, WHERE "GOOD FOOD AND FUN LURE INNOCENT CUSTOMERS INTO SOCIAL ACTIVISM"

The first stage in the process of leading a best-in-class values-based small business is translating your values into a business proposition. In this chapter, we'll review common myths and examples of how to capitalize on your values effectively.

## Why Are Your Values Important?

Leadership starts with you—who you are, what you care about, and what you want to see happen. Business is about the creation of value. Your job is to orchestrate how that value is created. So how can you create market value if you do not know what your values are?

The day you launch your company, you are its first product. You must sell your values, mission, and uniqueness to others. Rational market-value arguments are important, of course. But they alone won't do it. Whether you're trying to attract employees, customers, or investors, it's not just about the finance. It's also about the *romance*.

You need to engage people's emotions. To change their behavior, to get them on board, they must feel your excitement. When they feel it, you'll be on your way to creating value. Engaging people comes first. The actual product or service is secondary.

That excitement comes from you. It all starts with *actualizing* yourself, which is communicated through acts of leadership. What do you need to do? Let's look at three myths and their counterexamples for guidance.

## Myth 1: Leave Your Personality and Your Values at the Door. This Is Business.

### Truth 1: Bring All of You to Work—Your Values Produce Unique Value

If you leave what is most special about you at home, how can you make a unique contribution to the world? And who wants to live that way, anyway?

Fast talking, fast thinking, and always direct, David Berge, president of the innovative social venture fund Underdog Ventures, says that in hiring top people, "When someone comes to me for a job, the last thing I want to hear is how they want to do what I do. What I want to know is who they are, what they want to do, and how they think that would benefit the company. It might take them longer to find a job or start a company, but when they do, it'll be the right one."

In the days of the great British armadas, sailors lined up to go to the ends of the earth (literally, they thought!) for what was called the "Queen's Great Matter." They sailed for the "greatness of Britain and her Queen." What is your great matter?

The first question you must answer as a values-based leader is, *Why are we here?* Why are we doing this? Why are we giving our precious life energy or hard-earned money to this endeavor? An effective answer requires you to be personal and to touch people emotionally. After all, you want people as committed as you are.

Whom you attract will make all the difference to your future success. My values-based companies with the best, most innovative products failed, and those without great products at the start did well. Why? Because building a successful company is not primarily about the products. It's about the *people*. The right people can overcome the wrong products and even inadequate financing most times. And you get those people by being clear about why your enterprise is important and what are its values. Then you must act on those values. After that, you'll find the right products—together.

## Myth 2: You Need Business Experience and a Business Background to Run a Business.

### Truth 2: Study the Humanities and Get Service Experience

It's been said that building a business is like trying to ride a bicycle while you put it together. Values-based leadership is about offering something uniquely based on your values. You have the values, the uniqueness, so if the will is there, you'll learn what you need to know on the job. As the business grows, you'll hire expertise to fill in the gaps. *The key leadership skill is knowing how to build relationships with diverse groups of people.* What kind of background and experience best allow you to do this?

During the first half of the 1990s, I examined the characteristics of successful values-based leaders in the United States for a report to the United Nations. What I found was that many of those leaders had worked in less-developed countries or in disadvantaged areas in the United States for at least a year or two. From these cross-cultural service experiences, with access to limited budgets and resources, they developed competence in working with diverse groups of people, compassion for those different from them, and commitment to a business concept that serves humanity.

I believe that almost everyone I've mentioned in this book has that experience. For example, Linda Mason and Roger Brown, founders of Bright Horizons Family Solutions worksite child-care and early education centers, previously worked in the Sudan for Save the Children. They organized distribution logistics to get food more efficiently to outlying areas with starving children. That nonprofit work gave them the credibility to obtain venture funding from Bain Capital to start their for-profit enterprise.

CEO of Wild Planet Toys Danny Grossman is fluent in Russian. He served as a foreign diplomat in Leningrad and as a human rights officer at the State Department. Honest Tea CEO Seth Goldman worked for a year in China followed by a year and a half in the former Soviet Union. SVN co–executive director Deb Nelson was a Peace Corps volunteer in Cameroon, West Africa. And Jane Hileman, CEO of the American Reading Company, was a public-school teacher for twenty-eight years in our inner cities.

Regarding educational experience, a growing number of younger values-based leaders have gone to business schools. But first, many earned undergraduate degrees in language studies, religion, history, and English. The ability to communicate clearly in writing and speech is a critical skill for business leaders.

## Myth 3: Values Should Never Be Modified in Any Way.

### Truth 3: Values Don't Change, but They Do Evolve

Forgetting yourself in your work is easy. On a regular basis, it's important to stop and check yourself, your values, and your company's direction. Times change, and while values don't, how you *implement* them may need adjustment. If you don't adjust, you might find your work less satisfying personally and less profitable professionally.

This is particularly true if you take over a company you didn't found. While you probably buy into the values and the mission, they aren't exactly yours. Also, as time passes, they may need to take on a different form in the market. That's what happened when *Utne* magazine chair and CEO Nina Utne took over husband Eric's company in 2001.

Nina realized that the magazine had to be revamped, though it took her four years to get clarity, to overcome myth number 3. She explains, "I felt like I was entrusted with a precious resource and asked to steward it. But it took me all this time to realize that I've been curating *Eric's* twenty-year-old vision and values.

"Eric asked twenty years ago, 'What does the world need now?' It was a different information landscape. Today, there's even more clutter, and I believe what we need is different. We still need models of the way things can work, but more important, we need to encourage the evolution of the heart. Simply said, what we need is more love, sweet love." Nina has gone on to change the name and evolve the positioning of the magazine.

I've also found that it's rare that you start a company to accomplish a particular goal and end up doing exactly that. You may do more or less or something different. And it will always cost more and take longer than expected. You're never sure exactly what your world will look like when your company hits what Gary Erickson of Clif Bar calls that "sweet spot when the pieces just seem to fit together." Similarly, your values may deepen. For example, when Gary Hirshberg first joined Samuel Kaymen, who operated a small New Hampshire yogurt company called Stonyfield Farm, their mission was to help local dairy farmers, who were being paid less for milk than it cost to produce. Gary and Samuel wanted to pay them more.

These farmers are a proud lot, especially the independent farmers. So in order to pay them more, Gary and Samuel had to ask for more. They did. They asked for higher quality milk and cultures. That led to organic milk and yogurt, which led to a mission of increasing the production of organic foods worldwide.

Eric Friedenwald-Fishman's communications firm, the Metropolitan Group, serves social purpose groups. Originally, he served only commercial clients. Eric explains, "We liked being activists in college but didn't think we could do that type of work for nonprofits and actually get paid enough for it." After doing some free promotion for a few nonprofit groups, however, Eric was asked if he would continue on at one of them in a paid capacity. Still, it wasn't much.

With one year and $90,000 in sales under their belts, the four founders went on a retreat and asked themselves, "What work were you proud of this past year?" The top answers involved the nonprofit organizations, which had grown to provide nearly half of their sales revenue. When they figured out that the difference in profit margin between the nonprofit and the commercial clients wasn't very much, they focused on shifting their client base. They developed a fund-raising expertise as well, and today 100 percent of their clients are social purpose groups.

Turning values into value is a gradual process of finding your way, finding what products or services work, finding what stirs your passion, and finding what makes you feel good. Just be careful that you migrate *toward* your values, not away from them.

## Mistakes: What If You Don't Hold Your Values Sacred in Building Your Company?

It's better to fail trying to do what you really care about than to succeed at something else.

Make no mistake. It's not easy to succeed. It's hard to keep your values intact and be successful in the marketplace. One of the biggest decisions early on is how to handle the opportunities that come your way, each with its pluses and minuses, none with all the values and economics you'd like. Those decisions can make or break your business.

So much of leadership is saying no, not yes, of waiting for the market to catch up to you. So much of building a company is turning down deals, firing customers who aren't compatible with your values and social mission, and letting go employees who were with you at the start, who are your friends, but who do not have the capabilities required by a larger company. In the short term, however, financial needs can obscure everything else.

In the late 1980s, I started a company to develop computer-based interactive video programs on social issues. My concept was to sell these programs to corporations that would sponsor them in schools. Children would learn about human rights and the environment in fun, interactive ways. The sponsors would develop good public relations with the children, teachers, and parents.

After a few years of only sporadic sales, I met with a former marketing client who mentioned how difficult it was for employees to learn the values of the company. "It takes a dozen years for them to understand what we're really about," he admitted in frustration. "They don't read our corporate materials or watch the videos. We can't afford to send everyone to management retreats. What about your software, Mark? It does make the material more engaging. Do you think you could do something for us?"

I did. We became a provider of low-cost training programs on corporate values. Finances picked up, but it wasn't what I'd set out to do. I sold out a few years later. I had built a business that ultimately did not reflect my values.

As the leader of a values-based company, you must be true to your values, not just in speech but also in action—particularly when doing so is most difficult. Remaining true can require much patience and feel very lonely. But if you don't do it, who will?

## Doing It Right: Being True to Yourself

Tami Simon has not made my mistake. Instead, this book's title came from her interview as she explained how she translated deep personal values into a best-in-class company.

Tami is the founder and CEO of Sounds True, the largest producer of spiritual audio programs in the world. Tami is integrity. I mean "integrity" as psychologist Erich Fromm's defines it: "an unwillingness to violate one's own identity." Tami is Sounds True and Sounds True is Tami. In terms of values, they are one.

Tami is that rare blend of the highly competent and highly compassionate businessperson. Her commitment to her cause—*to disseminate spiritual wisdom*—comes through clearly. She is unusually direct. I've done business with Tami. She has said yes, and she has said no: both felt right to me. She's decisive yet inclusive. She makes tough decisions, yet she is fair. This is because she's so connected with what Sounds True is and is intended to do. And she works hard to understand who you are and what your needs are.

"As a leader," Tami begins, "you must be clear and authentic on why we are doing this, why *you* are doing this. I just don't get that excited about making money. *It's not where I spend my dream time.* That time is spent asking questions like, what will create the greatest shifts in consciousness?"

Tami believes she is standing for something that she completely believes in, something that she's willing to give her life energy to. And it fits her gifts and her abilities to contribute to the world. How did she get there? It took reflection, trial and error, and a wise adviser.

Tami dropped out of Swarthmore College after two years and spent the next year in India. She was a religion major, but she didn't want to teach. She felt that people didn't realize their connection to each other. "That's the fabric of existence, how our identities as sentient beings are interrelated with each other."

She returned to the United States and prayed every day for six months, looking for a sign of what she should do, what values she should bring to the world. She kept asking, "How can I contribute meaningfully?" She felt she was wasting all her education and talent.

She was never much of a reader but was always fascinated with speech and music. When her father died, she inherited $50,000. She was ready to lead her own life and wanted to do it with a level of passion and commitment that was extraordinary.

Tami had a radio show at the time, but she knew that wasn't her calling. One day she had a long conversation with Jirka Rysavy, the founder of office supplier Corporate Express and (in 1988) Gaiam, a healthy lifestyle company. He said, "You know what to do, Tami. *So why don't you put your money into yourself?*" When she left his office, "My awareness, my whole body shifted, and I knew that my work would be to create channels for disseminating spiritual wisdom."

How did she create the $12 million Sounds True while staying true to her values? "My fire attracted other people. When you have a strong vision, you can cut through the BS." Sounds

True's culture is like its product. It, too, has a truth-telling quality to it. Tami created a culture of truth telling where her job is to bring up "what I sense are the *'undiscussables.'* What's not being said? Where are the shadows in the office? You need to do that to get things done."

Tami brings out specific issues like "Why is this person making more than that person?" or "What are Tami's long-term plans?" or "This is a pet project of an author we like: is that why we're doing it even if it's not going to be a big seller?" She challenges herself to be forthcoming and keep no secrets because she doesn't believe there are secrets in a company. People know.

How then does Tami see her role as a values-based leader? "I simply help articulate the subtext. The way things feel between us is important to me. I can tell if people are upset, and I don't like to sweep things under the rug. I attract people who challenge me, who don't simply say yes. I reward disagreement, beginning with a simple 'thank you' to them."

Like Tami, Sounds True disseminates truth. The truth is that over twenty years, there have been bumps in bringing these values to market. Tami has had to get comfortable with how big a company Sounds True may become. She's had to become more aware of the business side of Sounds True, as values and value are not always compatible. At times, her work has felt like "being in a desert," so she has taken more personal time. For years she wouldn't leave the office if there were one more thing to do, one more call to return. No longer.

Similarly, Tami has been less involved in decision making over the past few years. Each person has a high degree of independence and flexibility at the company. She sees the company as a great opportunity for everyone there, a vehicle to bring their voices into the world. "How could I have a greater sense of contribution than I get through Sounds True?"

Tami's future may include more time spent away from the company, though her mission will remain the same. She will continue to put her values front and center in whatever she does. She will continue to be true to herself.

## How to Improve: Connect to More of Yourself

Nobody will love your business the way you do. Its spirit is your spirit.

Values are personal. Business is personal. The more you connect your business to yourself and yourself to the business, the more successful you'll be personally and professionally. You should allow no separation in policy or practice between how you act and how your business operates. But first, you need to answer the whys, whats, and hows of your business for yourself and others involved. That is, why are we doing this, what do we need to do, and how do we get it done?

Here are five questions to ask yourself to help you turn your values into value:

1. *How do you see what your company does as an outgrowth of you and your interests?* Can you list how the circumstances of your life led you to pursue current products and/or services? Can you connect what your company does with important experiences in your past? Can you explain the connection of your life with what your company does?

2. *What are the specific ways you transmit your values and commitment to others?* Does everyone concerned know what your company's mission and values are? Do they believe in them, and do you show that you believe in them, too, through words and actions? Do you compensate people in ways that support these values?

3. *What do you do when values-based decisions have con-flicting goals?* How do you make trade-offs among stake-holders who are impacted differently by a decision? If values conflict with financial opportunity, does a manager know what to do or does that person have to come to you? Are you consistent in upholding these criteria?

4. *How do you reevaluate your role in keeping your values and creating market value?* Do you have a regularly scheduled process by which to evaluate your role? Who runs the process? What changes have you made or are you thinking of making?

5. *How do you deal with the role of values in tough times?* How do you express your values in the marketplace when sales are down? How do you deal with a product failure that may be due to your values? How do you regularly reevaluate the role of values in your company and in the marketplace?

## Action Exercise: A Four-Step Process to Create a Values-to-Value Personal Inventory

Turning your values into market value is an iterative process that will increase your personal fulfillment and your company's competitiveness. It's important to regularly schedule a reevaluation process for these values and their implementation.

The following exercise is a personal four-step process that can be adapted for your company as well. For example, in the step involving passions and skills, you can substitute core competencies (or key business relationships). The exercise can also be used to communicate and discuss values among key company staff, customers, investors, and others.

I use Bright Horizons Family Solutions child-care and early education centers as an example to guide you.

**Step 1.** *Decide what your top six personal values are.* Get out a piece of paper, and think about your values for as long as you need. Make a list down the left side of the paper (leave room for a second column on the right). Feel free to use your experience to consider whether or not your values have been reflected in any past or present occupations.

**Example:** Respect, nurturing, trust, openness to change, balance, and sustainability.

**Step 2.** *Determine how these values are of value to your company.* Once you've determined what your values are, your second step is to create a value inventory for them. To the right of your list of values, create a second column for the value of your values. Your paper should now have two columns—one for your list of values and one for how each of those values can add value for your company.

In making your two-column list, you may want to think back to times when you weren't happy. What values did your job or your company not allow you to develop? Which were the values most important to your happiness and integral to your effectiveness? When you complete your two-column list, review it and make any necessary changes.

**Example:** Improved communication, high-quality care, credibility, innovation, good health and morale, and long-term performance.

**Step 3.** *Using the same process you used for values, expand your list to include your passions and skills as well.* If you like, you can do this on the same piece of paper, but most people like to use separate pieces of paper for their two-column analyses of their passions and their skills. You would then have three pieces of paper (each with two columns)—one for values, one for passions, and one for skills.

**Example:** Core competencies: good listening skills, experience at parenting, transparency, closeness to key corporate clients, patience as educators, and cutting-edge practices.

**Step 4:** *Combine these three separate lists of values, passions, and skills into* values-to-value *strategies.* Take the necessary time to develop three of your own values-to-value strategies, prioritizing them in terms of importance to you and ease of implementation in your company. Then put one strategy into action next Monday at work.

**Example:** Provide high-priced, high-quality services. Regularly update them by being knowledgeable about current research, and expand them to meet changing parent and client needs.

This four-step process creates a values-to-value list, expanded to include passions and skills (or core competencies or key business relationships) and then combined to develop three values-based personal (or company) strategies. The process can be time consuming, but I've found it invaluable. Work on the list over time, refining it as situations develop and change, and capitalize on these changes by consolidating them into your leadership plans.

## Summary: Turn Your Values into Value

This chapter introduced the most personal leadership practice, turning your values into marketplace value for your company. This is the starting point for building a business that reflects your values. Those values help you differentiate your company, but they will be challenged by short-term financial needs and an array of potentially distracting opportunities. How you navigate and negotiate the direction of your company by keeping those values and acting on them will determine your success.

It's important to bring to work your values, your personality—all of you—and to communicate clearly your responses to three questions: *why are we doing this, what do we need to do, and how are we going to do it?* These practices are important because mobilizing the right people to join you is more valuable than the products and services you offer.

The journey of Tami Simon, founder and CEO of Sounds True, was presented as an example of the first practice. Tami's lifetime interest in disseminating spiritual wisdom through the medium of sound and direct marketing led to the founding of Sounds True. The company has evolved in tune with Tami's personality and a maturing customer base.

This first stage is a gradual process of finding your way and discovering what works, seeing what stirs your passion and what makes you feel good. Just be careful that you migrate *toward* your values, not away from them. In the next chapter, we'll examine the second of the five practices of successful values-based leaders: walking toward the talk. This practice focuses on the second stage of values-based leadership: creating an organization that exemplifies the same values that you offer in the marketplace.

## 4

# Walk Toward the Talk

There's often a disconnect between being a responsible business externally and what it means to do that internally. The singular style of an entrepreneur conflicts with the ability to build a holistic internal culture to support it. The marketing skills used to build sales are different than the leadership skills needed to build the culture. It's a slow process that's a lot less tangible than what happens in the marketplace. It's hard to focus on *process* when you're used to focusing on *results*. It's hard to sit back and let other people do stuff you think you can do better.

JEFFREY HOLLENDER, FOUNDER AND CEO OF
SEVENTH GENERATION

The second stage in the process of leading a best-in-class values-based small business is institutionalizing values in your organization. In this chapter, we'll discover the common myths and review examples of how to build an organization that reflects your values.

## Why Is It Important to Walk Toward the Talk?

You launch a company that reflects your values. You want to do something special and satisfy multiple personal, financial, and social objectives. So you start hiring people who have those values as well as the skills you need. Meanwhile, you're focused on getting sales, raising more capital, and making sure everyone gets paid. But now lots of eyes are watching you in other ways, too.

73

Employees ask themselves, is this company really different? They want to see that your mission and values don't apply just out in the marketplace but also in daily operations. How will you make the mission and values come alive for each employee every day? It starts with making them come alive for you and your highest-ranking employee.

Now the executive vice president and partner, Judith H. Katz joined president and CEO Frederick A. Miller in 1985 at the Kaleel Jamison Consulting Group, which helps organizations unleash the power of diversity for business success and sustainable change. Since she was eighteen, Judith had felt that this was her calling: "As a child of Holocaust survivors, I have a deep connection with the issues of oppression and racism."

But working together hasn't always been easy for these two strong-willed executives. "Fred and I may be the longest running business partnership like this, working across gender and racial lines. [Fred is black; Judith is white.] At the start, we had many struggles as we each felt the other just pushed to get his or her way. Now, we've learned how to really listen to each other and use our differences as a strength. We've developed a close relationship with a lot of mutual trust and respect."

Still, it hasn't been easy, as Judith admits: "We all bring in our perspectives from traditional organizations—our mind-sets about hierarchy, leadership, trust, fairness. It makes it hard to practice what you preach. That's why we never say that we walk our talk. We just try to make sure we are walking *toward* our talk."

Judith and Fred work hard to model what their company preaches to its clients. As Judith said, the measurement standard is a direction, a *process*, like turning values into value. To understand the process of building an organization that breathes your values, let's look at three myths and some counter-examples.

## Myth 1: I'm the Founder, Not the Role Model; Building the Culture Is Not My Job.

### Truth 1: Everyone Watches Your Example as the Embodiment of Company Values

Frequently, business leaders don't realize the impact their words and actions have on others, especially staff. That effect is amplified by word of mouth. For example, Kinko's employees knew of founder Paul Orfalea's "surprise" store visits almost before he knew! And if he made just one slightly negative comment during his visit, store personnel were crushed. All 23,000 Kinko's employees would know what he had said within hours. But if his comments were positive, store employees were energized for months.

I've often wanted to leave the people part of my companies to someone else. I've learned, however, that I can't abstain from my role in the company culture.

During a difficult time, I sought advice from a CEO I respect. She listened and responded emphatically: "Yes, Mark, you have to let go of control, but that doesn't mean you shouldn't be *involved* with your employees. How you spend your time signals what you think is important in the business. And since you're spending no time with them, how do you think they feel?" After her advice, I was soon taking time at the home office to meet with employees in *their* offices—a further indication of my respect for them and their work.

You're the keeper of the values and the mission, in full view all the time. Your employees will see all the contradictions. If, for example, you say they should spend time with their families and not work late, then why are you in your office at 9:00 p.m.? One of my clients was the CEO of a global service company. She'd rarely stay in her office after 6:00 p.m. as she wanted to signal to her employees that she supported a balanced life. Rarely did she call them outside of their business hours unless there was an emergency. Truth be told, she'd work through the night at home and travel 250 days a year. With offices in forty-six countries, it was always business hours somewhere! But she was meticulous about not letting her home office employees see or endure her extra work time.

Like it or not, you set the tone. If you work late, working late is a value of the company. If you treat people with respect, that's a value, too. Staff will watch everything you do. Whatever the rules are, they apply to you more than anyone else.

Business operations and procedures also express your values. CEO Jim Kelly started Rejuvenation, a period-authentic lighting and house parts company, with a code of behavior and respect that permeates the 200-employee culture today and got an unexpected payoff. Jim was a hippie in 1977 and questioned every business practice. For example, he decided that "we would be fair and cost based in our pricing, not charge what the market would bear. I also decided that we'd report all of our income, something most small retail businesses don't do. We modeled honesty in everything we did—even when it cost us money. So when we hired people, many from the inner city, we never had any problems with stealing or skimming. It also meant that when we wanted to get a loan from the bank, we had tax returns with profit to show them!"

The advantage of a small business is that you, the founder, are there. As Babson College leadership professor Allan Cohen says about how a founder can create the culture, "You're the one who can pull people beyond their narrowly based interests, communicate the vision so people can say it in their sleep, build a team as committed as you are, and put the toughest issues in front of your team and make them deal with it." How you deal with people is a daily example of how you care about something beyond yourself.

## Myth 2: What Matters Is What You Can Measure; My Job Is to Increase Sales.

### Truth 2: Your Most Important Work, Building an Organization, Can't Be Measured

One of the things I like about capitalism is that it has a score-card. It has agreed-on accounting principles, relatively rational capital markets, and rules that cover most business situations. In every company I've started, I've been the initial sales team. I brought in the business and figured that the rest would take care of itself. It didn't.

Clearly, without sales you have no company. But getting sales is not the same as providing values-based leadership. Leadership helps build relationships to create an organization that will last. I didn't appreciate the importance of that immeasurable distinguishing characteristic called company culture or my role in it.

Greg Steltenpohl, founder and former CEO of Odwalla, the leading supplier of fresh juice in the United States, explains that leadership is a design function: "As architect Bill McDonough points out, 'Who's really the head of a ship? It's not the captain. It's the designer. The captain simply manages through the design.' So don't glorify the old head-of-the-ship model. Instead, values-based leaders need to create organizational cultures of *distributive* leadership."

Creating a values-based leadership culture is different from a leadership-*driven* culture. Rather than dazzle everyone with *your* performance, ask yourself how you can build the competence of the team—its motivation, its commitment, and its sense of meaning at work. If you don't do it, you'd better have a partner who does. I've seen several partnerships work this way. For example, the self-effacing, whimsical founder and chair of Calvert Group, Wayne Silby, generated innovative product ideas as partner John Guffey managed a cast of talent to support Wayne.

Calvert's innovations were made not only in financial services but also in how the company formed teams. According to Wayne, "We found smart, resilient people. We developed a great rhythm in the company." When they faced a crisis, they had a lot of confidence that they could deal with it. They were resourceful and could rebound from mistakes quickly. Wayne and the team didn't know it was possible not to bounce back.

Calvert had a culture of constant, intensive, face-to-face, honest conversation that allowed Wayne to receive important criticism and refine his ideas before bringing them into the marketplace. Listen to Wayne's reaction after he and John sold most of the company: "I realized I had sold a team. I recognized that our most valuable assets weren't these innovative financial service products, these 'assets.' We had built this incredible team and culture filled with 'go-getters,' who later on started their own businesses. The team, the culture, was our biggest asset."

Several summers ago, I participated in a research project with Goldman Sachs on the top five predictors of increased stock valuation over five years for service organizations. The number-two predictor was a sense of excitement, a buzz you could feel in the home office. We didn't use the word "culture," but if you look at the interview write-ups, that's what it was: an enthusiasm, a special camaraderie shared from one department to another.

## Myth 3: Values-Based Leadership Is Primarily about Your External Impact on Society.

### Truth 3: Values-Based Leadership Is about Your Impact on All Stakeholders

Values-based leadership is about how you choose to express your humanity through your business. Every decision you make in designing your organization, its products, its external relationships, its capital structure, and its business partnerships is an opportunity to express your values.

I remember asking Ben Cohen in 1990 to talk to SVN members about what Ben & Jerry's did not do well. Although the company was renowned for giving 7.5 percent of pretax profits to community projects, Ben noted that while it did a good job of sharing its profits externally, it had yet to do as well for its employees. Getting people all jazzed up over a cause is the easier, more visible work outside the company. Walking toward the talk on a daily basis is the less visible, quiet, but equally important inner work.

In the early 1990s, the executive director of SVN at the time, Patricia Novak, asked me to visit with a man she said was the best model of a values-based leader in the country. That man was Elliot Hoffman, cofounder and former CEO of San Francisco's Just Desserts. With a bakery plant located in the inner city's enterprise zone, Just Desserts and Elliot were known for their community work. But it was the quiet respect, democratic benefits, and care given to his diverse group of 250 coworkers, who spoke seven different languages, that garnered Elliot even more fame. At the time, several presidential candidates had made a campaign stop at Just Desserts, proclaiming, "This is the face of America. And this is how an American business should be run."

Values come in many flavors. For some, the values embedded in the products and services offered are most important. For others, it's how the company operates as a community and structures its ownership. Still others look at how they support external social and environmental programs. Just don't forget that the sustainability of all those values comes first from that set of beliefs shared inside your company—your culture.

### Mistakes: What If You Don't Walk Toward the Talk?

"If I have anything to share, Mark, it's to make sure you *don't underestimate the things you can't count.* The most important thing you have at your company is your culture, through which you engage your values and inspire action."

Those words are from Jay Coen Gilbert, cofounder of AND 1 and subject of the June 13, 2005, *Sports Illustrated* eight-page cover story, "How a Tiny Shoe Company Happened to Start a Basketball Revolution." Ironically, the magazine came out the day that Jay and his partners announced the sale of AND 1. Rapid growth had weakened the culture, not only because of what happened to the people already working there but because the hasty hiring of new people never gave them a chance to be imbued with the company culture. Jay and his partners lost control of AND 1's culture and then the company.

Four years out of college, Jay went into business with his best friends. The culture was strong the first six years. "We were each other's families. We went to school together, started AND 1 together, experienced our twenties and thirties together. Girlfriends became wives, jobs became careers, and couples became families."

They created a cooperative environment based on a positive tension between fearlessness and humility, dreaming of building the number one basketball company and helping teenage boys in inner cities. They had a culture in which you checked your ego at the door and everyone was receptive to constructive criticism. "We knew that the best team wins. We hired a lot of smart young ballplayers who realized that AND 1, too, was a team sport. AND 1, the underdog, was taking on Nike!"

Growth accelerated. They went from 50 to 150 employees in eighteen months as sales shot past $200 million. Things began to unravel. Jay reflects: "We felt we could do no wrong. Complacency replaced healthy competitiveness, fearlessness became cockiness, and humility became arrogance. We lost our edge."

In the midst of this growth spurt, venture money "allowed the founders and other shareholders to take real money off the table," and they launched a dot-com division "with other people's money." The management team and the founders were split between the two divisions. They realized too late that their sales momentum had masked all the underlying issues, like taking care of the culture. They now had two divisions competing aggressively instead of cooperating. "We never realized that the culture of our family business was going to become like Cain and Abel," muses Jay.

It's easy to take your eye off the ball, away from the intangibles that are the company's glue. Jay and his partners had lost sight of their roles as leaders, the keepers of the values. They had stopped asking the hard questions of themselves and of others.

In retrospect, they should have hired a top gun to run the dot-com division instead of dividing their management team and creating internal competition and pressure from what was essentially another business—one they didn't know how to run. By being so focused on the adrenaline of growth, size, and speed, they paid scant attention to what had gotten them there in the first place—a "kick-ass" team.

Jay and his partners needed to take a step back and assess what was happening. They could have relaunched the company and taken on new roles better suited to the company's size and their personal interests. That's what SVN board chair Mal Warwick did with his company. Let's see how he struggled, evolved, and eventually succeeded at walking toward the talk.

## Doing It Right: Providing Daily Meaning

There's a big difference between providing great benefits and understanding *how to produce fulfillment for human beings.*

In addition to the company that bears his name, Mal Warwick & Associates, Mal is the founder of three other companies that bring fund-raising and marketing services to environmental, progressive political, and human rights organizations. Now free from daily operations, he travels the world to teach fund-raising, principally in developing countries. A whirlwind of activity, Mal is frenetically committed.

He admits that he never thought about leadership until recently. He started his namesake company in 1979 and began hiring full-time staff in 1983. He didn't see himself as a good leader or manager. His company grew 100 percent a year for several years in the 1980s, a growth spurt for which Mal felt unequipped: "I had no idea what it meant to lead a small company, much less be 'values based.' I had the strategic, creative, and technical skills to be a well-paid consultant but no experience or training in management, much less leadership."

He quickly learned that his leadership position gave his actions an importance he didn't know he had: "I was truly a workaholic, insensitive to the needs of a staff that wanted some balance in their lives. It took me a long time to understand that my role required me to think about how I might inspire or deflate the people around me."

Mal realized that he had a multifaceted role as teacher and mentor. He had to be more careful about what he said and think more about how to motivate and support staff. As he spent more time out of the office, these roles took on a greater importance. After all, management is about what happens when you're around. *Leadership is what happens when you're not there.*

In the 1980s, Mal was a self-described "control freak," a handicap of most founders. He started off doing everything from opening the envelopes and licking stamps to analyzing results for his clients: "I knew I could do it better than anyone else. No one was as competent as I was. I could have made a lot more money solo, but I wanted to achieve more than I could do alone—and I wanted my work to go on after me."

Mal joined SVN in 1990 and talked with fellow CEOs about success and failure. It was a profound experience: "I concluded that I wasn't successful. I didn't have the kind of organization that could carry on. I saw that to support advocacy work at nonprofits and foster the kind of social change I wanted, it would require a lot more hands on the oars."

Mal's challenge was not simply about moving from managing to motivating. It was more about values, something he hadn't paid attention to beyond delivering a superior product with great customer service to clients whose work he cared about. He did have employee loyalty as his staff was dedicated to the clients and inspired by *them.* But his staff didn't have those same kinds of feelings about the company. Mal needed to bring those values inside his organization.

Mal asked himself how he might build that commitment through policies and practices. He spent a few years learning about profit sharing, creative benefit programs, and environmental stewardship. But his personal values and politics got in the way.

In many ways, 1988 was a high-water mark, at least for Mal. The company raised $7 million for Jesse Jackson's presidential campaign and got a lot of press, but the campaign almost bankrupted the company. The day after the election, Mal had to lay off forty of his eighty-seven people.

Mal had some personal problems, too, and went into a depression. He cut his salary to $25,000 and became largely inactive in the company from 1989 to 1994. He did some individual consulting and writing but had little energy for the business. When the succession of CEOs he promoted from within each encountered resistance from employees, Mal was forced to confront the issue of why he wasn't involved and what it would take to get him to come back to full-time work.

Mal gave his board of directors his conditions: "I told them that I wanted to put into place a comprehensive set of socially responsible business practices that would make our company per se motivating for the staff, just as our clients' work motivated us." He had put in place good benefits, but he needed to do more.

The staff wanted a strong profit-sharing plan, a voice in management, and more environmental leadership. These priorities led to the election of staff representatives to the company's board and to intensive environmental and energy audits. The audits have made the company a showcase for service companies.

As for the profit-sharing plan, Mal proposed to the board that half of the company's pretax profits be set aside each quarter, with 20 percent of that half (10 percent) going to charitable contributions selected by staff. The remaining 40 percent would be divided up largely on the egalitarian basis of one person, one share. What was the board's reaction? "Well, the board flipped out," Mal chuckles knowingly. "'We could have a cash crunch!' I told them that they could be right, *but it wasn't worth keeping the company alive if we couldn't make a statement about social responsibility.*" They ended up settling on 45 percent of profits going to the plan, with 35 percent going to the staff and the same 10 percent to charities.

Mal returned to astonishing results. From a base of no profits, the first-quarter checks were $30 per employee. By the fourth quarter of the new profit-sharing plan, the checks amounted to $2,000. The company has been profitable ever since. In a peak year, a staff member making $20,000–25,000 in salary received an additional $8,000 from profit sharing. The plan jump-started the change in culture the staff had been waiting for.

In 2002, Mal began the transition from sole ownership to employee ownership. An ESOP (employee stock ownership plan) was put in place. By 2005, 10 percent of the ownership was in the ESOP and another 24 percent among key employees—a democratizing of ownership Mal intends to continue for many more years. Mal knows that it's never too late to reinvent your brand of leadership and reignite your company.

As Mal's story shows, few small business founders think about what it means to be a leader or what their role is in creating a culture that produces fulfillment for others. Becoming more of a teacher and less of an expert consultant and salesperson requires a shift of attention from consumers to employees. But if you want to make a difference in your industry, you must walk toward the talk and bring those values inside your organization on a daily basis.

## How to Improve: Give Up Control and Stay Involved

Starting a business and building a company are almost completely different tasks. Creating a culture in which employees are aligned with your values and mission is the biggest challenge for most values-based small business leaders. But to magnify and sustain your impact, especially after your tenure, you need to move your attention from customers and investors to the culture and your team.

Here are five questions to ask yourself to help you lead your company's culture:

1. *How do you translate your values into the company culture?* What assumptions do you bring from past experiences about leadership and culture? How do you acknowledge the importance of a culture that reflects your values and a team that helps you "do your thing"? What skills have you developed to be a better leader of company culture?

2. *How have you let go of control as the company has grown?* What do you delegate and what do you not delegate? How do you nurture leadership and create a sense of ownership? When you're not around, do your managers manage and your employees work as effectively—or better—as when you are around?

3. *Do you provide a fulfilling environment?* Are you careful not to grow your business faster than your employees can handle? How do you ensure that employee turnover doesn't negatively impact your culture? Do you treat your employees as well as you treat your other stakeholders?

4. *Are you aware of the impact you have on your employees?* How would your employees describe you? How do you ensure that what you do and what you say are not taken out of context by others? How do you model the values you espouse to people at work and in your personal life?

5. *How do you ensure that your company culture stays on track and keeps your values?* How much time do you spend attending to the culture, to people matters? Do you deal with the tough issues? How is your leadership reviewed on a regular basis?

## Action Exercise: A Three-Step Process Using the "Four Ps" to Walk Toward the Talk

This exercise will aid you in building your company's culture. I use information about President Steve Piersanti's evolving job at Berrett-Koehler (BK), the publisher of this book, to help you apply the exercise to your company.

A good starting point is to answer the questions in the preceding "How to Improve" section, asking yourself each time, "What can I do to improve?" Please also use your responses to the first action exercise on translating values into value. This exercise will help you assemble that information in a form you can use on Monday morning at the office.

You may be familiar with the marketing leadership process of using the "Four Ps" model to make decisions. You look at product, price, promotion, and placement to gauge the effectiveness and consistency of marketing campaigns. Similarly, values-based leaders can use another four Ps as a tool to organize information. This tool will help you gauge how you are doing and what you need to do better to create a supportive company culture. You look at your impact on *people, processes, products, and profits.* (It is assumed that your impact on the *planet* is evident in each of these areas, although some people like to make this factor explicit as a fifth P.) However you do your assessment, it's important to use a process that can readily involve other people and honest input. Once you have made a company-wide assessment, then you can focus on your role in improving your current position in these four areas.

Step 1. *Make a general assessment of your company's current mission and culture.* Create three columns on a sheet of paper. Use the first column to write down your mission, the second for your description of the current culture at your company, and the third for any gaps between the two. Feel free to ask for help from staff.

To be clear about what I mean by "culture," it is the shared beliefs, customs, practices, and expected behavior of people in your organization. For example, someone might say, "That's a BK person" or "That's the BK way of doing things." Substitute your company name for BK, and write down what each statement means.

**Example:** BK's mission is to "create a world that works for all." The BK culture is democratic and collaborative. When the company was founded in 1992, Steve wanted the organization to include explicitly all stakeholders, not just employees.

**Step 2.** *Put the information from step 1 in a more detailed form that you can act on.* Take a second sheet of paper and title it "Culture Carrying Out the Mission." Make four rows down the left side, titled "People," "Processes," "Products," and "Profits." Then make two columns across the top. Title the first column "Need to Do" and the second "My Role."

Now fill in the first column. For example, what do you need to do better on the people side of your business to fulfill your mission? How can you better reflect the culture required? Don't feel you need to comment on both culture and mission equally.

**Example:** At BK, *products* need to "help us to integrate our values with our work and work lives with the hope of creating more humane and effective organizations." *Processes* need to promote collaborative decision making that recognizes the importance of each individual. For example, all twenty-one BK employees are involved in title and cover selection of the books to be published, through the use of e-mail, blogs, and other technology. BK hosts authors' days, an annual authors' weekend retreat, and community dialogues, and in November 2004, BK held the first Positively MAD (Making a Difference) conference, at which authors presented new ideas. In these ways, the interest of all *people* involved with BK can be honored. Moreover, as *people* include all stakeholders, BK's board consists of two BK managers and an employee, an author, a supplier, an investor, and an author-investor. In 2005, ownership consisted of all twenty-one BK employees (through BK's employee stock ownership plan) as well as several dozen of BK's authors, several dozen of its customers, and many of its suppliers and service providers. The use of profits is under employee-directed consideration.

**Step 3. *Fill in the four boxes of the column "My Role."*** After you fill in the four boxes, prioritize the four areas of your involvement and list three specific things you can do Monday morning to help move your company culture toward your company mission.

**Example:** Steve's job resides in asking the question, how can we manage for the benefit of all? "It's tough to do. There's no pat answer. Primarily, I concentrate on how we treat people, even in bad times. We're designed to have lots of ways to connect with each other and benefit all. I keep looking for new ones."

Steve is particular about selecting only *products* he believes contribute directly to BK's mission. He continually works hard not to dominate any of the *processes,* an ongoing "experiment" in running a publishing company collaboratively. He hires *people* who are strong decision makers but who have the patience required to work collaboratively. And he is one member of a committee that decides what to do with company *profits.*

This three-step process gives you an overview of the gaps between what you say your company should do and what is being done and then a more detailed way to explore how to create the type of company you want. By focusing in the third step on your role in creating the culture to support your mission, you can develop a clear leadership plan that communicates to staff how they can help you walk toward the talk of your company's mission and values.

## Summary: Walk Toward the Talk

This chapter introduced arguably the most difficult leadership practice, building a company culture that reflects the values you espouse in the marketplace. The personal marketing skills required for starting a company and the leadership skills required to build an organization are different. It may be that no one does what you do and no one can do what you can do. But you may have to stop doing what you are good at and do what your company needs most. That can be difficult emotionally as well as practically.

If business success is to be personally fulfilling and professionally sustainable, you'll need to focus on internal processes as much as external results. This transition from the fast-paced competition and the tangible market scorecard to the slow-paced cooperation and intangible process of building an internal culture requires patience.

Moreover, everything you say and do will be scrutinized, particularly as a values-based leader. The impact of *how* you spend your time, *how* you say things, *how* you treat people, and *how* your actions match your words is greater than you may know. You're the architect of your company, with a great opportunity to design the way a group of people can accomplish results no one could attain individually.

The journey of Mal Warwick, founder and CEO of Mal Warwick & Associates, illustrates the growing pains of developing a values-based culture. Mal's dedication to the mission has shaped his ability to make the difficult transition from consultant to leader.

Like the first stage of values-based leadership, walking toward the talk is a gradual process—an unending but exciting journey to build a business. In the next chapter, we'll learn the third of five practices of successful values-based leaders—communicating with care—which is the most important "how" behind the practice of walking toward the talk.

# 5

# Communicate with Care

> Kate [wife and manager] gets people to open up
> and find solutions. She's taught me how to be-
> come inquisitive, rephrase things back to people,
> ask probing questions, and be discerning. I'm
> learning how to tell *what's a burning bush and
> what's a land mine* in deciding when to intervene
> and when to just listen. For me to do that, I must
> bring out my emotions.
>
> DARELL HAMMOND, COFOUNDER AND CEO OF KABOOM!,
> THE NATIONAL $18 MILLION NONPROFIT CONSTRUCTION
> COMPANY THAT BUILT 850 PLAYGROUNDS IN A DECADE

The third stage in the process of leading a best-in-class
values-based small business is communicating with the care required of leaders. We'll learn about common myths and review
examples of this core leadership practice, including how to
change people's behavior by connecting with their emotions.

## Why Is It Important to Communicate with Care?

You're trying to establish your values in the marketplace and
build a culture in the workplace. What makes that happen?
Communication. In my previously mentioned research project
with Goldman Sachs on the best predictors of increased stock
valuation, the number one predictor was the quality of intracompany communication channels. And who's at the center of
your company's communication efforts? That's right, you.

The *Encarta World English Dictionary* states that communication is "the exchange of information between individuals by
means of speaking, writing, or using a common system of signs

93

or behavior" or "a sense of mutual understanding and sympathy." You're aware that listening and "walking in someone else's shoes" are important. You recognize the value of having people feel comfortable speaking up honestly, but do you appreciate the determinants and power of leadership communication?

## What Determines Communication Effectiveness?

George Bernard Shaw quipped, "The biggest problem with communication is the illusion that it has occurred." Communicating with care starts simply with showing how much you care. When you ask a question, are you sincere? As twenty-six-year-old social innovator Julia Davis once told me, distinguishing a year in Russia from her life in the United States, "In Russia, when people asked you, 'How was your day?' they meant it. They wanted a real answer. And they would listen. It was a stark contrast to what I was used to in the States."

When you speak, *what* you say is less than 10 percent of the communication. Nearly 40 percent is *how* you say it and the rest is the *context,* including your body language. Ask yourself, When people talk to me, am I actively listening, being *present,* without multitasking (such as sorting my e-mail at the same time)?

## Do You Appreciate the Power That Surrounds Leadership Communication?

As mentioned in the last chapter, you may not realize how much more communication occurs than you're aware of—especially surrounding you. You speak to one employee and everyone else finds out what you said. Your every act is scrutinized.

You're the model in your organization. With that power comes the responsibility to be sensitive to your impact on others. For example, in his desire to be honest and transparent, Eric Friedenwald-Fishman, CEO of the Metropolitan Group, would bring up his concerns as they happened, almost thinking out loud: "I'd tell everyone we had to buckle down, when as their leader, I need to be a bit of an actor. It's my job to take them beyond the moment, to provide inspiration and be sensitive to their needs and concerns."

## Myth 1: As the Company Grows, I Need to Focus on Efficient Communication Methods.

### Truth 1: Increase Your Effectiveness by Being Personal, Individual, and Challenging

Founder and former CEO of Robinson's Jewelers, a national chain of jewelry stores, Larry Robinson told me that the most important thing that he did was to handwrite thirty thank-you notes each month to employees who had done outstanding work. Conversely, I stopped working for a company when a new CEO with a logistics background let go 100 senior managers who had each served the company for over ten years—with a single typed form letter.

Communication is personal. What you can do with one handwritten letter, one word, one look, one smile, or one minute of listening can bring a company together or break it apart. As your company grows and people advise you on how to manage your time better, the tendency is to limit these personal moments to interaction with top managers only. Nothing could be a bigger mistake.

At Calvert Group, the nation's largest family of socially responsible mutual funds, veteran CEO Barbara Krumsiek oversees 200 people and $10 billion in twenty-nine funds. Barbara likes to "have nothing on my desk that I'm responsible for." She focuses her time and energy on bringing together the efforts of her staff and "the work on their desks" so that all the pieces of the business work smoothly as one.

Barbara surrounds herself with the best people and makes it easy for them to get the support they need from her. She also knows her staff *individually* so that she can adjust her methods of communication and motivation for each person. In her words, "We have smart people doing some great things. It's my job to make sure they are taken care of. To do that, I communicate with them in the ways that work for them. That might be in print, by e-mail, one-on-one, or in small groups. I also make sure to say the important things more than once and in multiple ways."

Her biggest mistake is at times not asking enough questions, especially tough ones. "You believe everyone will come to you," Barbara admits. "Particularly if you consider yourself a values-based leader, you may not challenge people enough, be a bit 'soft.' It's not a sign of a lack of support to challenge someone." This can also be an issue with friends at work. Just as with the value of compassion, challenging someone early on in their employment can be best for all concerned.

Communicating with care also doesn't mean that everyone will agree with you. Barbara observes that "technology has flattened organizations today. Our relationships have become more like those with peers. I don't think we all have to love each other. It's important to be independent and have our own expertise and our own styles."

Barbara tolerates a high degree of disagreement: "'Collegiality' doesn't mean I make decisions everyone supports, either. What's important is that everyone feels that they were heard and that I communicate my desires and decisions to them in a way that most effectively allows them to hear what I'm saying."

Of course, Barbara also supports her employees, even outside of work. For example, when an executive had a milestone birthday, she flew up and back from Washington, D.C., to New York that night to be there. This effort is all part of how she takes care of her staff, something she feels she could do with 400 people just as well as the current 200.

## Myth 2: Effective Communication Is the Art of Persuasion for Mutual Agreement.

### Truth 2: Speak the Absolute Truth and Confront Tough Issues Intelligently

Founder and president of the National Foundation for Teaching Entrepreneurship (NFTE), Steve Mariotti is used to dealing with tough inner-city teens. He's unrelenting about the importance of speaking and acting on the absolute truth—however painful that may be: "You can package whatever you have to say in a nice way, but never hold back. If you're thinking a thought you think is true, assume that it is and act on it. When a conflict isn't resolved, it'll come back in subliminal ways to hurt you and the company. Resolve it as soon as possible. If you don't set the tone for people to say what they're really thinking, you'll have lots of dysfunctionality in your organization."

Steve realizes how difficult it is to deliver tough news or deal with potentially uncomfortable conflicts, but he feels "it will be such a relief later." He believes you should start with saying something positive, then convey the negative, and end by repeating the positive things or offering a possible solution.

It's also important to allow people to disagree respectfully, to create an environment that promotes personal and staff honesty. Adrienne Maree Brown, a twenty-six-year-old leader of a national network of young voters in low-voter-turnout communities, uses the "fierce conversation model" to make sure everyone has a say. It also helps her stay in tune with what's going on.

With a lot of young employees and temporary workers, Adrienne feels like a traffic cop. She uses the fierce conversation model each week to help people bring up difficult subjects. In her words: "Often when you're the leader, you get talked about. People aren't sure how to bring things up. We all sit together, have a moment of silence, and pass around a talking stick. Then someone says something and we leap into it without judgment.

"A lot of what comes up is what their working styles are. Real specifics like how they like to be evaluated, how they feel they can be most creative, and what are their hours of greatest productivity. It allows me to bring up honest feedback so I can help them feel good about working here and give them the opportunity to do their best."

A real test as a values-based leader comes when you have to be honest and confront people with whom you have a personal relationship. I know several married couples who colead their companies. How do they stay honest, work out conflicts, and keep their businesses and marriages healthy at the same time?

Before coleading Bright Horizons, Linda Mason and Roger Brown coauthored a book and served as codirectors in the Sudan for Save the Children. They developed a set of principles, particularly around how to give each other critical feedback, that echo Steve Mariotti's technique. Linda explains: "We always do it in a constructive way and often use *humor.* We dispel a lot of tension with humor. For every piece of critical feedback, we'd put it between two nice things. I remember a number of times when I was reading our manuscript that I'd search furiously to put a check mark beside something I liked that Roger wrote when I knew I had some criticism coming up."

Also as Steve suggested, they don't let concerns build up. They learned in the Sudan to debrief after every key meeting— they would talk not just about the content of what they'd said but also about the *process,* even when it sounded silly. When they don't agree, they become enormous talkers. Extremely tuned in to each other, they each know when something bugs the other and don't let it simmer. Roger's more natural at this, but he's been patient as Linda has worked hard to get better.

Linda would often say that something was not important, that it was just a "grain of sand." But Roger persisted, according to Linda: "He'd say something like 'It's okay, even if it's just a grain of sand,' and we'd laugh. It became a playful little game. At times, we'd stop and do a little dance. We now have probably a dozen games that we use to break the tension, relieve the stress, and communicate—truly *connect*—always making sure the other is okay."

Linda and Roger are both stubborn, independent leaders who don't always agree. But they make sure their relationship is nurtured and use humor and play to keep their priorities clear and the truth front and center.

### Myth 3: Great Communications Are Great Speakers First and Foremost.

#### Truth 3: Be a Great Listener First, Then a Great Communicator

The importance of good listening skills and sensitivity to people's needs can't be overstated. How do you know what to say unless you've listened first—and continue to listen?

The first step to becoming a better listener often involves dealing with your ego. Social venture capitalist David Berge speaks of the critical importance of continued listening during highly pressurized situations that leaders often face; for example, when negotiations between you and important clients or investors are getting sticky. David remarks that while the clients or investors usually know they may not be 100 percent correct, they may communicate as if they believe their perspective is right no matter what and then stop listening. He advises: "When it gets most tense, good leaders don't lose their perspective or take disagreement personally. If investors say their company is over-valued, some leaders react by thinking 'They're not valuing me.' They'll lose the direction of the conversation by delivering a diatribe about how wrong the investors are in how they value *my* company or *me*.

"Good leaders respond, 'I think *x*, and you think *y*. Let's figure out a way to make this work based on looking at results.' Or they take a deep breath, say something like 'I don't agree, but let's move on to other important areas and keep the communication lines open.' They don't get hung up on who's right and who's wrong."

How do you learn these skills? To slow down, Steve Mariotti suggests putting your hands out of sight and squeezing them together until the other person finishes speaking. He allows that even if what's being said is time consuming, the consideration you show by listening patiently builds rapport, gets people motivated, and often provides you with important information you may have otherwise missed. How do you do that for your company?

Always interested and interesting, Alisa Gravitz is the executive director of Co-op America, a national membership organization that addresses the economics of sustainable consumption, green business, and socially responsible investment. In 2005, Co-op America had 3,000 businesses in its green business network alone and over 70,000 people in its green consumer network. The organization operates as a worker-member cooperative with democratic decision-making processes.

Listening is clearly a critical task in a grassroots organization like Co-op America. How does Alisa improve not only her skills but also those of her fifty staff members? Since they wanted to offer an accessible workplace for everyone—consistent with the values of social and economic justice they promote in the marketplace—and since the neighborhood includes a university for deaf students, they made a commitment to the deaf. Alisa notes, "*Whenever you bring diversity into your organization, you get back many times over what you might think you're giving.* With two deaf staff members—Kitty, who has been with us twenty years, and Diana, who has been here eighteen—all of us have to understand more deeply what communication is about and practice what we learn."

Co-op America brings in a sign language interpreter for staff meetings, which means unavoidably that one person speaks at a time in all the meetings. The staff have learned how to listen better and how to have a conversation in which everyone participates. Aware that English is often a second language for deaf people, Alisa admits: "We often design systems assuming that the users all have English as a first language. Here, we need to be sensitive to different kinds of people, beginning with language proficiency and accessibility. We find ways to allow people to preprocess things."

For example, Co-op America's staff often have meetings with lots of reading and writing content. They also now have a preparatory meeting beforehand so they can go over questions people have about the material they will address in the main meeting. They began doing this for their deaf staff only, but now a number of other staff members come, too. This allows them to be better listeners when they hold the main meeting.

"We have learned how people learn, communicate, and listen differently," states Alisa. "So now we've put in place a robust set of policies to make sure we fully engage everyone. All of this happened because of our commitment to the deaf community."

## Mistakes: What If You Don't Communicate with Care?

Trying to communicate with care in all you do and say is a daunting task. There are so many little ways you can mess up. That's why honesty and transparency are very important. You're going to make mistakes. You'll say or do the wrong thing at times. Recognize it, admit it, correct it, and move on. You can even hold a company celebration when you mess up unintentionally.

The issue can be as simple as where you hold a company event. A financial services CEO chose the Ritz Hotel for an executive retreat. The Ritz was new and had offered a deal less expensive than the local Holiday Inn. However, the CEO didn't tell his managers about the deal. The company was in severe cost-cutting mode, and these managers had been asked to cut their departments' costs to the bone. Disgusted by this apparent extravagance and other insensitive oversights, over half of the managers left the company within the next six months.

Some values-based leaders expect employees to work for below-market salaries. One such company told my MBA students who were applying for a job after graduation that they should accept 20–30 percent less to work there. Now, I'm not talking about bootstrapped young companies or nonprofit organizations where low pay is an economics issue. I'm not talking about leaders who decide to keep a low ratio of highest to lowest paid employees. This company was paying low rates because "we can get away with it." If you have this attitude as a leader, you will create a second-class organization because you're communicating that status to your employees.

However, I think that the most dangerous mistakes can often be the most subtle—those "little things." For example, Steve Mariotti was the only one of the seventy-five people interviewed for this book to mention "courteous" as one of the top four traits of a successful values-based leader: *Always be courteous.* It's a mistake to bring irritation and mean-spiritedness into a conversation. Rise above situations, stay calm, and treat people with common courtesy even when angered. Otherwise, they won't hear you. Your tone of voice is important, too. The main mistake people make is being rude when under stress. Be Churchillian."

When Steve told me this, a scene immediately flashed in front of my eyes: A number of years ago, I facilitated a meeting between two CEOs of multibillion-dollar companies for a possible partnership on a significant amount of business. The press had been eagerly following the story, but what the reporters didn't know was that the deal was dead less than a minute after the two men met.

I was escorting the visiting CEO, who'd flown across the country for the meeting. When we arrived at the host company, he was not met by the other CEO but by an assistant. She brought us up to the CEO's office. The CEO simply stood up from behind his desk to shake the visiting CEO's hand. *He did not even move from behind his desk.* He did not offer any refreshments or ask about the 3,000-mile trip. He went right to business with pointed questions. Needless to say, he received sarcastic replies, which infuriated him.

Beyond the importance of common courtesy, smart leaders are knowledgeable about the people they meet and tailor their communications accordingly. In this instance, the visiting CEO was very attuned to the courtesies commonly offered a guest. This fact was not well known because he was press shy, but it would have been easy enough to find out. The host CEO could not have cared less, and it showed. He thought that he had the upper hand and was using it, but instead, a deal he wanted badly never stood a chance. The visiting CEO had decided immediately after the "greeting" that he would not do business with this man.

An extra moment spent with someone, acknowledgment of a sensitive matter, or going a little out of the way are all small acts of leadership communication that can make a big difference. They make me think of social investment expert Amy

Domini, who brings in a massage chair every Friday for her thirty KLD Research employees. "They get a kick out of it way out of proportion to its cost. It shows I care."

## Doing It Right: Becoming More Mindful

President Mark A. Finser leads the $90 million RSF (Rudolf Steiner Foundation) to help people understand how money relates to their values. His calm outer demeanor belies his fierce inner desire to extend RSF beyond its historical limitations—its narrow definition of what activities RSF could engage in, as invoked by Rudolf Steiner in the late nineteenth century and applied by the original founders of RSF since the 1930s. Mark "refounded" RSF in 1984, became its president in 1992, and since 1997 has been pushing the foundation members to become innovators in social finance.

Today, RSF is growing at a 60 percent annual rate, providing community investment, loan and grant funds, philanthropic management, and advisory and educational services in sustainable agriculture, children and education, and economic and social renewal. A spiritual practitioner, Mark has led RSF to examine the deeper, cutting-edge issues that surround the spiritual significance of money and the redistribution of wealth. For Mark, communication is not as much a matter of emotions as it is of spirit.

Mark has put in place a number of policies to help integrate spirit and matter in his quest to transform the world of money. He asks questions like *"How do we communicate in a way that incorporates spirit in everything we do?"* He believes that if we communicate in this way, respect for each other will not be far behind.

Before every business meeting, he holds a moment of silence for people to experience whatever they wish. For Mark, it's a profound experience: "You can feel the energy shift in the room.

It also sensitizes us to each other. At RSF, we're connecting people who have resources with people who are in need. As an intermediary, the first question we need to ask ourselves is, *How can I help you?*"

Mark engages in other practices as well to help staff be more mindful. For example, he asks staff members to initial every page of the financial statement sent to their investor clients. He has learned that "just the act of thinking for a second about a client before mailing out his or her quarterly statement can be personally meaningful. It's also a way of showing clients that we care and respect their investment with us." RSF receives significant positive feedback from clients about this practice.

Mark also helps borrowers be more mindful. Since borrowers see RSF as a source of funding, once a year they receive a list of those who made their loans possible. Mark wants the borrowers to see that their funding comes from real people. They tell him later that when they're paying back their loans, they realize that they're allowing their investors to put that money into supporting someone else. This approach respects the borrower, who's empowered to be a steward just like the investor. "If one side is concerned about the other, we're all more mindful of how our actions affect the other," offers Mark.

A new employee's paycheck is another opportunity to communicate with care. RSF employees are paid on the first and sixteenth day of the month. When people join RSF, they start on one of those days so that they'll receive their paycheck for the next two weeks in advance. "It surprises them, but we know that many have been out of work for a while so things are probably pretty tight. Ultimately, I want to separate their work from their compensation. I don't want them to work for a paycheck but for the work itself."

For Mark, the "devil is in the details." He wants to incorporate every staff member's spirit in everything they do. As a leader, he needs to constantly attend to his own inner growth: "By attending to the 'being' and not just the 'doing' side of my leadership, I help ensure that we are led to achieve a much greater level of efficiency for the organization. The integration of doing and being increases productivity for me and, by my communicating it to others, for them, too."

Mark's message is great advice that requires a lot of personal will to carry out. No one said being a values-based leader would be easy. But if you can work on being mindful of how you communicate to others and what is communicated, that's a great start.

## How to Improve: Increase Your Sensitivity

*Communicate, communicate, communicate.* Communication is at the heart of all relationships; it's at the heart of leadership. Increasing your sensitivity to the perceptions you create in all aspects of your life at work is not easy. If you can, work on one aspect of your awareness at a time. If I had to choose one to begin with, it would be to learn to listen fully without judgment.

Here are five questions to ask yourself to improve your communication skills:

1. *How can you improve your listening skills?* Do you remain courteous and respectful when you'd rather be doing something else? If not, how do you think you may be irritating others (e.g., multitasking, talking over people, using distracting body language) and could change? How can you improve your ability to know what isn't being expressed?
2. *Do you know how your employees like to receive different types of messages?* Do you know what messages to deliver publicly versus privately for each employee, whether to meet with staff in their offices or yours? How

do you know your message has "gotten through"? Are you careful about your tone and use of e-mail?

3. *How do you deal with the tough issues?* Do you deliver bad news or ask challenging questions as soon as possible, before larger problems loom? How open would your staff members say you are to criticism? How do you exhibit "tough love" with the emphasis on "love"?

4. *Are you clear and consistent?* How do you ensure that it's easy for your message to be transferred correctly to others? When you're working on a speech, how much time do you spend on the speech versus preparing answers to questions (where most leaders slip up)? When you're under stress, what aspect of your communication skills could you improve?

5. *How do you spend your time?* How might you change the amount of time you spend one-on-one versus in meetings, on your work versus helping others with their work, at the company versus outside the company? How do you know when to give someone your time and when not to? What do you communicate about how your time is best spent?

## Action Exercise: Communicating across Differences

An important part of communicating with care is learning how to reach a satisfactory solution for all when points of view are different. This skill is most evident in negotiations, but it is useful in any communication with divergent viewpoints.

This exercise comes from Terry Mollner, founder and chair of Trusteeship Institute, Inc., a think tank and consulting firm founded in 1973 that focuses on the development of socially responsible businesses and spiritually based enterprises. Terry first used this exercise during negotiations between Ben & Jerry's and Unilever in 2000.

Terry is a practitioner of transforming communication through what he calls "three-dimensional" thinking, In short, you are asked to use two questions:

1. What is the *truth* here?
2. What is for the good of all?

Terry calls traditional thinking and communication "two dimensional." They focus on the typical competitive win-lose paradigm, as in sports. You and I communicate as two people with divergent interests, resulting in one winner and one loser (the two dimensions).

Terry believes communication should move from being competitive to being collaborative so that people communicate as members of the same team. This happens when priority is given to the good of all involved. Terry calls his method of transforming communication "three dimensional." In this type of communication, a third party is acknowledged, thus adding a dimension: the party of "us" ("you," "me," and "us" are the three dimensions). An example is when a husband and wife talk about their children. They're giving the priority to the "us"— what's of mutual interest.

The question Terry asks business leaders is, "How do you communicate, negotiate in particular, in ways that help put you on the same team, making the whole the priority, not one side or the other? It's not just a win-win. It's bigger than that. It's not just what's best for the two of you but for others in the community affected by your decision."

To get two sides to think this way without knowing it, Terry uses the two questions about truth and the good of all. He asks everyone to stop everything, to sit and be silent for a few minutes, and to consider the two questions.

Try Terry's exercise. Take a Monday-morning issue at your company and check your communication with the relevant employee, investor, customer, or supplier. Write down what you feel is being communicated before and after, not just in what's said but in how it's said, in body language, and the like. Note what worked well and what didn't and how your listening may have been changed by the two questions. Feel free to share your observations with each other. The exercise should make you more sensitive to the relational nature of communications.

Terry summarizes his experiences after using the two questions: "After a few minutes, people began to restate their positions by integrating the position of the others into their comments and giving priority to their common ground. The two questions helped them identify more with the whole by going a little deeper into themselves and communicating from a different, more humane, place inside them."

## Advanced Tip

Three aspects of leadership communication, developed originally by Aristotle for Alexander the Great and called *ethos, logos,* and *pathos,* use character, logic, and compassion to create a common ground among people. Usually, people focus only on the logic (logos) when communicating and forget to connect by being personal (ethos) or expressing empathy (pathos). Terry's exercise challenges you to be more personal and compassionate, which usually helps bring people together.

**Example with pseudonyms:** A child under the care of a nanny died, and the company that provided the nanny was sued. The company president's first public speech after the tragedy originally began, "We at First Corporation are sorry about the death of the Smiths' baby. We deeply regret their loss, but . . ." Later, after working with a leadership communication coach, his speech began, "I, John Jones, father of three children, can only imagine the pain that the Smiths are going through. My staff and our entire company join me in deep regret . . ."

Do you see the difference? If you like, use Aristotle's understanding of leadership communication when you conduct Terry's exercise.

## Summary: Communicate with Care

This chapter introduced the leadership practice of communication central to building a successful values-based company and culture. Excellence in leadership communication requires that you deepen your sensitivity to how you interact with people and how you're perceived. In that way, you can connect more effectively with people with a range of operating styles.

Only a small part of communication is what you say. Most leaders don't understand the amount of communication that goes on around everything they say and do. You have the daunting task of being sensitive to all of it, and you need a process in place for honest feedback and for how you respond to that feedback.

It's important to communicate personally and individually and to be willing to tackle tough issues quickly and honestly. While listening skills are essential, the use of humor, staying even tempered under stress, and simply being courteous are highly effective aspects of successful communication.

The leadership of Mark A. Finser, president of RSF, offered an example of how being mindful of the many details of how we communicate with each other can make a difference. Mark's leadership in incorporating spirit into everything he and his staff do leads to exemplary customer service and employee fulfillment.

The values-based leader communicates personally, logically, and empathetically to build relationships and a culture that's adaptable to changing times. In the next chapter, we'll learn about the fourth of the five leadership practices: facilitating personal growth. This practice focuses on how to innovate and increase effectiveness through personal and organizational transformation.

# Facilitate Personal Growth

Each of us has a spark of life inside us, and our highest aspiration ought to be to set off that spark in one another . . . At Bioneers, personal transformation begins with the lifting of spirits just by the act of coming together, recognizing we're not alone. You can see people changing as they're touched by the power and possibility they feel emanating from the group. That's the power of Bioneers to effect personal and global transformation.

KENNY AUSUBEL, FOUNDER OF BIONEERS, AN ANNUAL ENVIRONMENTAL CONFERENCE

The fourth stage in the process of leading a best-in-class values-based small business is facilitating personal and, thereby, organizational growth. You'll learn about common myths and read examples of the practice of change, starting with your organization—and you.

## Why Is It Important to Facilitate Personal Growth?

If nothing else, business is about change. To be successful, companies can't become too attached to any product or service. They need to be nimble and self-teaching. "Change or die" is the acknowledged motto. That's your best bet, too. If you don't listen, if you don't adapt and grow, how will your organization remain competitive? How will your employees be challenged toward greater personal fulfillment and professional contribution if you don't lead the way?

Values-based leaders direct their energies toward people. They see business as a living organism, a change agent for society at large dedicated to serving people. For example, what would Julius Walls say about how he leads his business? He's the CEO of Greyston Bakery and senior vice president for business at the Greyston Foundation, an integrated network of companies providing a comprehensive set of resources for the homeless and people living with HIV/AIDS. With twelve minutes on *60 Minutes* and a profile in *Fortune* magazine to his name, Julius would like to see that fame translated into more sales for the bakery so that more lives can be saved. You see, Julius doesn't view business the way most of us do.

In a few minutes, Julius can change your thinking and reframe your questions about what business and leadership are about: *"Business is a force for personal transformation.* My job is to help people grow. When I take care of them, they take care of the product, and the product takes care of the profit."

To make this philosophy work, Julius recognizes that the needs of the whole person must be attended to before a person can deliver his or her best to the business. Employees can access services available through Greyston such as child care, job training, and outpatient care. Julius oversees the bakery, or, as he sees it, "I give resources and access to opportunity for people who don't normally get them. Our people are the rejected parts of society. They have no access to power. We're here to employ them and serve them. We strive to help them gain confidence and grow." For example, new Greyston employees must pass a probation period, although Julius calls it the "apprenticeship program," which offers cash incentives for learning new skills every two weeks.

Having trained originally for the priesthood, Julius constantly challenges himself on how he puts his spiritual beliefs into action as a business leader. He reflects on how he can become a better Christian and businessperson as he meets daily demands. He relies on clarity, consistency, and compassion in setting the rules of his leadership—rules "intended to help each individual reach his or her potential." He's just trying to change the world through business, one person at a time.

## Myth 1: The Organization Can Change, but I Don't Have To.

### Truth 1: Organizational Change Begins with You

I don't know about you, but I've always felt my leadership skills were just fine and that I didn't really need to change a thing. I didn't have time for all that reflection. I was too busy moving my company ahead. So when I first joined SVN, I wrote a column for the newsletter on what I thought members should do to move SVN ahead.

When I received the newsletter in the mail, I saw that next to my column was one on the same topic written by Mel Ziegler, the founder of Banana Republic. Mel trashed me. He said that members should do nothing. Either he was being funny or he was simply an idiot, I thought. A dozen years passed before I realized what Mel was saying.

SVN was a young organization back then, loaded with high-profile leaders who all had their own ideas on what to do. Members had meetings to collaborate and establish a direction. Our attempts were fruitless. We never did as Mel suggested. We never examined who we were and what personal changes we needed to make first so that SVN could then reflect those changes as an organization.

Our wasted energy was most notable in efforts to transform the SVN membership. I chaired the membership committee in the early 1990s, when SVN's lack of diversity became evident. Members were predominantly white males of similar ages, but we wanted to attract more women, people of color, and young leaders. We were able to attract and retain leading women, but we experienced difficulties and embarrassing failed attempts with the other groups. What did we need to do? We needed to change from the inside, starting at the top.

Leading this entrepreneurial, fragmented organization was a nightmare. And few members wanted to serve on the board. SVN floundered until the last several years, when a leadership transformation took place that in my opinion has led directly to transforming the organization's culture and increasing its diversity. The leadership change has forced SVN to focus on building relationships among diverse groups of people.

As Joyce Haboucha of Rockefeller & Company, Inc., the SVN board chair at the time, will tell you, most of the board was against this change: *coleadership.* "Impossible. It'll never work. You need one person running things and making the decisions," Joyce heard. That was the essence of the board's reaction to Deb Nelson and Pamela Chaloult's proposal for coleadership of the network, something that had never been done.

"We'd already been doing it informally for four or five months," recalls Pamela. So they wrote up a plan for the board on how their coleadership relationship would work and went through a strategic planning process in January 2002. The board accepted their proposal—and got more than they bargained for. "That coleadership model is a good lesson for the world," notes Joyce. "We gave them simple rules and hired a facilitator to keep things on track. And we got two strong women with two sets of skills instead of one."

As they worked out their relationship, the personal transformations for the more business-minded Deb and the more spiritually oriented Pamela served as a microcosm of the changes needed in the network. "We wanted to move from being *servant* leaders to *serving* leaders," Pamela remarks. "We'd been so fragmented by responding to every request that we weren't serving the organization as a whole. As our coleadership model transformed, so has the network."

SVN was scattered, and often new kinds of people felt left out, which is why they didn't come back. "It wasn't about saying yes to everyone," observes Deb. "In a coleadership model, you have to be very deliberate about the ways you communicate and collaborate. Similarly, our network had to be focused more on collaboration to attract people from diverse backgrounds."

SVN had to be more sensitive to how to accommodate and learn from member diversity. At four conferences, Deb and Pamela held impromptu sessions for all members to discuss issues of diversity and inclusion related to the network and members' organizations, with suggestions implemented by the next conference. More specifically, closer attention was paid to respectful interaction and dialogue among members.

For example, the "Men's Circle" ran into problems with the younger new members. In the confidential men's forum with no judgment allowed of any comments, older veteran members were comfortable teasing each other publicly. Younger new members took umbrage and spoke up. The men's group responded by reorganizing from one large group into several small ones, with an opening and a closing session for all the groups together.

"We haven't cracked the code," admits Deb. But SVN has become a more diverse, inclusive network that represents broader constituencies and has a clearer direction than it did previously. It all started when two people changed how they and ultimately their organization modeled leadership.

Change begins inside your company, not outside it. We often focus our energies on how we want to transform the marketplace, not realizing that transformation can happen only *after* we've made the prerequisite changes in the way we operate our business. If we want to have a more diverse customer base, for example, we first need to focus on having a more diverse organization. And as with any successful change initiative, it all starts at the top—with how we operate as leaders.

## Myth 2: Fear and Crisis Best Motivate Personal Transformation.

### Truth 2: Inspire Transformation by Evoking Joy and Hope through Stories

When you facilitate change, it changes you as well. How do you want to be motivated to change?

Speaking for myself, I like to be motivated by a desire to keep doing a better job for people I care about: my team at work, my family at home, and my friends in the community. I mean no disrespect to leaders like Intel CEO Andy Grove, who feels people are best motivated to change by paranoia. But even Bill Gates, renowned for his long work hours driven by fear that some small company will beat Microsoft to the market, says that he motivates people to work and grow best by his *enthusiasm.*

Geralyn White Dreyfous is the executive and creative director of the Salt Lake City Film Center. The Oscar-winning executive producer of Zana Briski's documentary, *Born into Brothels,* Geralyn believes that leaders facilitate transformation by telling stories that are easy to identify with, emotionally resonant, and evocative of positive experiences that paint a picture of a better future. As Geralyn sees it, "You're only as successful as the story people are going to step into. What are the stories you tell to lead? Those stories will tell people who you are. A good storyteller will *shift something in you.* It's a way to deal with the complexities of life and of running a company. It lets you clearly state a perspective that leads people to action and change."

Probably everyone agrees that people don't change until they have to. In my work with career transitions, I often say that people don't change until the pain of not changing is greater than the fear of change. Is that the only way? No. For example, appealing to the child within might motivate personal change. One example is close to my heart.

In the early 1990s, my two daughters started reading. It was a pleasure to read with them before bedtime, but many weekends we read (and colored) something different: Ben & Jerry's annual report. Unlike other annual reports at the time, this one talked about the company's product and social mission and did so in simple language with cartoons and fun activities. My children learned that business could do good things. They also learned that good businesses recognize what they did that was not so good so that they can work on doing better. And they even learned about balance sheets and income statements.

Ben and Jerry *treated us not as wallets but as people.* We were not only financial stockholders (which our girls became upon birth—their one stock!) but also part of the company. We attended their stockholders' festival, of course. My daughters are now in their teens and socially aware. I feel that it's due in no small part to these change agents who reached them through story and gave them the opportunity to color in their own way what for many others is the black-and-white world of business.

## Myth 3: Transformation Should Be a Comfortable Process.

### Truth 3: Learning and Growing Can Be Painful but Educational Experiences

It's true that a leader's job is to provide a supportive environment that helps people manage stress in times of change. But it's also true that the process should stretch people out of their comfort zone in the best interests of personal and corporate growth. You even may want or need to change your own style of work, yet more often than not, it's difficult to do so on your own.

It's said that there's no constituency for change. No one wants to change. You're forced into it by past circumstances or a current loss. But that experience gives you the opportunity to grow in ways that help you become a successful values-based leader. Personal transformation depends on acknowledging those "teachable moments" when they appear and taking advantage of them to create the change you want to see. That's what Melissa Bradley did.

Growing up in an apartment in a single-parent family, Melissa learned early on how hard it is to access capital for college. When she saw what her mother, a forty-year-old black woman with a child, went through economically and socially, she knew what she wanted to do with her life: "I wanted to shift the paradigm of capitalism so that people of color are not all on the bottom. I promised myself that I'd level the playing field so all people have equal opportunity and parity in this country."

Today, Melissa is the president of New Capitalist, which provides business development and capitalization assistance to emerging and social entrepreneurs. In the past six years, New Capitalist has facilitated over $20 million of investments, with average returns on investment of 25 percent. New Capitalist also measures "SROI," a social return index that includes measurement of increases in self-esteem, job creation, individual and community wealth, tax savings, and social support systems.

What has Melissa learned as an African-American woman starting businesses in her twenties? What can we learn from her about facilitating transformation?

Melissa started her first financial services company at twenty-one. She went for a Small Business Administration loan and was told that she had three strikes against her: "You're twenty-one, you're a woman, and you're black." As Melissa wryly offers today, "This was no news to me." She continues: "It was a huge blow. I'd left traditional business and gone on my own to get some control over my life, and someone else had taken it away."

Without access to capital, Melissa grew a national company of educational and financial consultants, leading fifty-two employees by the mid-1990s. She learned that personal transformation starts with how you look: "I had to change my appearance. I was leading people older than me so I did 'the look': glasses, suits, and a briefcase. Still, they didn't trust me." So Melissa debriefed everyone about everything she did, in person and on a Web bulletin board. That worked. "They felt more confident about me and that they'd get paid each week!" she acknowledges.

Melissa's major lesson on how to facilitate personal transformation came when she was pursuing a large contract. The company employees felt it would be best for someone older to visit the client, but since this first meeting was only for a letter of intent, they agreed that Melissa should go. The minute she walked into the senior executive's office, however, she knew something was amiss. He greeted her with, "Wow, I mean, I just expected someone different."

Melissa thought about what he meant by "different." As she did, she saw a diploma on the wall from Georgetown University, her alma mater, and tried to make a connection. It didn't work. Finally, he confessed: "I was expecting someone white." Surprised that he actually said it, she relaxed into a casual conversation about Georgetown.

She thought they were doing well until he said, "You remind me of my daughter. She's young and naïve and wants to do all these great things in the world, but you need to buckle down and earn your way up. It's the school of hard knocks." Now her *age* was a problem. Melissa went over her company's history, the $4.5 million in annual sales, client references, and even 360-degree evaluations of her leadership. No luck. With fifteen minutes left, she asked what she could tell him that might change his mind. "Forget it," he replied. "I decided you weren't right when you walked in the door, but I wanted to give you a second chance." She left fuming but without a word.

When she returned to her office, she decided to write him a letter challenging him. He actually called her back: "I did some digging at Georgetown. I didn't think I could trust a young black woman. Look, I'm third in charge here. Maybe I made a mistake, but I'm trying to move up and I was afraid to present you to the company."

Melissa is a master at handling these opportunities, one encounter at a time, to transform them into something positive. At that meeting, however, she realized she had no leverage. She took it as an educational moment to begin her own transformation. Today, she can use her experiences as learning moments for others, too. Her advice: "You don't combat ignorance with ignorance. You don't add fuel to the fire. Now that I'm in my thirties, I've found my voice and have learned that with ignorant or disillusioned people you shouldn't try to convince them. That won't change them. You need to *educate* them with facts, figures, and examples—in my case, regarding competent and successful African-American leaders. That's what I do in my organizations today."

Since then, Melissa has served on twenty-six boards, including those of SVN and Georgetown University. Usually the only black person on a board, she starts cultivating a black replacement, as soon as she joins. "That's how you can create change. One person, one company at a time, by educating them and have them feel as comfortable as possible with it."

## Mistakes: What If You Don't Facilitate Personal Change?

Some people and their organizations don't change and they do just fine, they say. Some people don't want to change and aren't forced to do so. That's fine, too. But then what are you doing reading this book?

Life is change and change is difficult. Personal change requires that you let go of many assumptions, beliefs, and even values you may have held since your birth. The most common difficulty I've experienced is having to go against common wisdom, which may come from friends, family, or peers.

When I started teaching at Harvard Business School, I was young and looked it. I needed to grow up in many ways. I knew that. But rather than finding my own way, I listened to others who cared about me but whose ways weren't my ways.

For example, I was told to have students call me "Professor Albion," whereas I liked to be called "Mark." I was told that if I made a calculation error during a class discussion, I should not admit it. When I "grew up," I used humor to turn those errors into positive class experiences, and I was called "Mark."

It's not that you shouldn't listen to elders, mentors, or parents, but personal change requires you to go deep inside yourself and find your own way. Otherwise, how can you get others in your company (or in my classroom) to do the same? Still, when you're also asked to leave what you know for what you don't know—even to leave *people* you know—that's tough. That was the dilemma facing Van Woods.

The most exciting interview I conducted was with Van Woods, a man on the go. Van was shopping while we were talking. Every time his cell phone ran out of juice, he'd run into a nearby store, buy another battery, and call me back. That frenetic pace is typical of the life of a social entrepreneur committed to building his family business and his community. But to do that required Van to grow on his own in other directions.

Three generations of Woodses and great employees have made Sylvia's Restaurant of Harlem a renowned African American–owned business. Established in 1962 with a seating capacity of thirty-five, Sylvia's now occupies most of a city block, with a capacity of 450 people, and serves patrons from around the world.

There's always been a connection between Van's mother, Sylvia, and the community. Van glows: "'Right on to you, Sylvia,' they say in support of her. That's because she's a hard worker, not pretentious. The black community respects someone who made it and worked hard for it, ground it out, and didn't have it given to them."

Sylvia does more than that. "She won't let people go hungry. If people don't have money, she gives them food. She also gave people jobs. She took them in when they were down on their luck. People remember that and talk about it."

"The Queen of Soul Food," Sylvia established quite a legacy for Van—a legacy started by her mother, who taught her, "Freely give and freely you will receive. But be careful not to give *all* of yourself."

"Doing this with my family has been a true blessing," confesses Van. "I'm part of something that was started by Mom and Dad, and I've had the chance to expand it. I grew up in it, and they planted the seed in me to make a contribution. Now my children are growing up in it, too."

As the oldest of four children, Van has led an aggressive expansion, buying up the block of real estate for the restaurant, opening a second Sylvia's in Atlanta, and launching a line of food and beauty products. When Sylvia's first opened, Van was motivated by a story his father told him about Howard Hughes and how Hughes took his father's small hardware business and made it into a big conglomerate of businesses old and new—a real social innovator. Van was even more motivated when he had a brief but inspiring talk with Reginald Lewis, the first black entrepreneur to lead a buyout of a billion-dollar company

(Beatrice International Foods). But to be successful, Van would have to change himself and those around him.

His first problem was being overly optimistic so that by 1994 he had $700,000 in debt for the food products that hadn't sold as quickly as he had hoped. He counted on his relationships to find what he needed, people and money, but his journey took him through many disappointments. He felt he'd given all of himself to his community, yet nothing was coming back. Then, inadvertently, Van made something happen.

Being a lifetime member of the Democratic Party, Van became tired of being taken for granted as just another black supporter. He took a strong political stance in a statement he made at a political event held at Sylvia's Restaurant. It got a lot of media attention as well as attention from his community. Van recalls, "It took a long time and a lot of courage for me to do it, but I was so frustrated, I felt that I needed a major change on the political and business level." It also meant that he'd be supporting a white candidate for state office over a black candidate.

For Van, that one act led to personal changes, and a new community appeared to him. He met bankers, food distributors, and CEOs of other food companies who had been invisible to him before. They all found ways to help Van. And it seemed that after one good relationship blossomed, that person would introduce him to another. What did he learn?

"I learned first and foremost not to make assumptions about people or answer for someone but to ask. Consciously or not, you make judgments about who people are or should be, about who's interested in what you're doing and who's not. So you don't ask. I never thought bankers at JP Morgan would be interested in Sylvia's. But they were." Van also learned that he needed to grow personally before he could grow his company. His very public stand caused him lots of personal heartache but surprisingly led to the personal and subsequent professional growth that he needed.

Today, Van's community is larger. His old community has embraced the expansion, and he has added a new community of supporters. All because he learned to *ask without judgment* an important personal growth question: "Will you help me?"

## Doing It Right: Growing Your Company by Growing Intimacy

Let's look at the thought process of someone who, like Julius Walls, CEO of Greyston Bakery, uses business as a source of personal growth that changes the way people work and live.

"Our relationship with people, animals, and nature is more important than dollars," proclaims former SVN board chair Judy Wicks, cochair of the national Business Alliance for Local Living Economies (BALLE) and founder and CEO of Philadelphia's White Dog Cafe, a $5 million restaurant famed for its outreach programs. "That's why I'm happy to not only give my advantage away to competitors, but I'll even educate them."

That's Judy speaking about her cruelty-free menu. When she discovered how pigs were treated inhumanely, "like machinery," as they were raised and prepared for slaughter in the factory farm system, Judy took pork off her restaurant's menu. Once she found a local farmer who raised free-range pigs, she not only purchased pork from his farm but loaned him $30,000 for a larger refrigerated truck so that he could deliver to other restaurants in the city.

Rather than keeping her cruelty-free menu as a competitive advantage, Judy provided consulting for other restaurants on how to buy from local farmers so they could copy her and increase demand for humanely raised local pork as well as other healthful farm products. Many competitors followed Judy's example and made the switch. She then helped increase the supply by raising $40,000 to improve the breeding stock and provide fencing and shelters for four more local pig farmers who switched to free-range practices. The press, politicians, consumers, and other business leaders commended Judy publicly, while more customers flocked to her restaurant.

Today, this cruelty-free initiative is now part of a full-fledged nonprofit organization, the White Dog Cafe Foundation, which runs a program to educate other restaurants and assist pig farmers and manages other community programs as well. Judy funds the foundation with 20 percent of cafe profits, customer donations, and grants from local foundations.

That story captures Judy's thought process. I have known her for ten years, and when I think she has exhausted the possibilities of how her solitary restaurant can impact individuals and the community at large, she keeps coming up with more creative ways to go deeper. Her creative strength comes from one source, *intimacy*: "I know all of our 100 employees, our suppliers, and our regular customers. I couldn't do this with more than one restaurant. That's why I've stayed with one—*to maximize the quality of all my relationships*. In this way I can create more personal and social change by developing this model than if I had a franchise with many locations. And this is more fun!"

Judy's leadership goes well beyond her company to her concern for the survival of our species, which depends on inner growth, partnership, and a sense of belonging. She advocates: "Many CEOs run their businesses like a one-night stand. People are buying from nameless global corporations with low prices. There's no feeling of intimacy or community, just of loneliness, separateness. We have lost our sense of *place*."

Judy thinks of her relationships not only in her company and with her customers but also with all parts of the local community—suppliers, competitors, and retailers in other trades. She wants to build a sustainable local economy that benefits all and is not concerned with growing the White Dog bigger and bigger.

Going outside your company and going deeper are results of how you think about growth and measure success. Judy challenges conventional thinking: "We have to change our measure of success away from continual material growth. When we grow our companies larger, we use up more natural resources and add to the concentration of wealth. Even with ESOPs, wealth remains in the hands of the few. *We must focus on other forms of growth if we're going to grow a more just society.*"

What has made the White Dog so successful is that the growth is internal. It's within Judy and in her one place of business. As she says, "We go deeper in our creativity and individuality, rather than larger with conformity. We are growing consciousness and relationships—all the things that make life interesting—in a way that is sustainable and enjoyable for us and those we touch."

In my experience, any company that can reduce people's loneliness and give them a sense of belonging can change the way we do business and be financially successful. You do that by deepening your relationships, or as Judy challenges, "Can you hear the cry of the pigs in their crates? Can you hear the mother cows crying for their calves? You ask, 'How can my business be based on the suffering of other creatures?' Constant growth for increased profits is destroying life. We need to build an economy based on compassion for all of life. I'm not interested in growing a national brand. I want to spread my business model and work collaboratively to build a sustainable local economy. Let's lead business to change the world we live in for the better by *spreading models, not brands.*"

## How to Improve: Attend to Inner Growth

You are in the business of change. You transform products or services in ways that offer unprecedented value. You hire a group of individuals and form a community with a set of norms and values used daily to operate your business. Then you have to make the numbers work, overcome problems with suppliers, customers, and so on. It's easy to lose sight of the inner work you need to do to accomplish your personal and professional goals.

Here are five questions to ask yourself to help you focus on personal growth:

1. *How do you define your business and its mission in human terms?* How do you balance developing employees with building market share and profitability? How do you relate personal growth to company growth? How do you define success for yourself, your staff, and your company?
2. *What do you see as your responsibilities to your employees?* What is the role of personal development in your company? Do you help employees learn and develop as they want to, even when it does not directly benefit your company? What's your role in developing employees?
3. *How do you improve your abilities to lead your company?* What are the areas you most need to work on to be a better leader? How do you develop yourself not just intellectually but emotionally and spiritually to improve your relational abilities and personal happiness? What activities outside of work help you be a better leader at work?
4. *Do you motivate by fear or by joy?* What story do you tell of the future of the company and your employees' role in it? How do you help employees feel comfortable taking risks and failing? How do you take mistakes and turn them into "teachable moments"?
5. *What is the role of diversity in your company?* How do you ensure that all are welcomed? How do you lead differently with a more diverse group? How do you

leverage the talent of people of different ages, genders, races, religions, ethnicities, or lifestyles?

## Action Exercise: Transforming Relationships

This exercise is a good way to open the doors of transformation at the individual, organizational, and societal levels. Drawing exercises are used in many companies to help people understand more about themselves and fellow employees. They also help individuals develop their emotional intelligence, which facilitates group bonding and productivity.

This exercise, called "Soul and Animals," is from Gillian Caldwell, executive director of WITNESS, which partners with human rights defenders, training them to use video to document abuse and create change. Companies often use this kind of exercise once a month or any time new staff come on board.

In seven years, former attorney Gillian took WITNESS from a one-person, $100,000-budget organization to a nineteen-person, $3 million-budget organization. While she then felt that the organization was big enough, she wanted to build local branches to expand WITNESS's impact and visibility.

Gillian knew she could be demanding and impatient: "The real challenge is to create a culture that can do this type of work. To do that, we need to feel comfortable with each other, grow together, and be connected. We need to understand each other's strengths and weaknesses—intellectually, emotionally, and spiritually—starting with Gillian."

The exercise asks you to answer two questions:

1. If you were an animal, what animal would you be and why?
2. What does your soul look like? Draw a picture if that's easier than words.

The work should be done in pairs, preferably of people who don't know each other well or who have had some conflicts. Take your time. Process is important, too! When you're done, each person describes his or her partner's soul and animal to the group.

**First question:** If you were an animal, what animal would you be and why?

**Example:** Gillian's group of thirteen women and two men that day included two dolphins, three cats, one lioness, one elephant, one cross between an owl and a turtle, one horse, one wolf, one wood monkey, one orangutan, and three "we weren't exactly sure what they were."

"We had a good laugh. It gave people an opportunity to talk about themselves in not only intellectual terms but also relational terms. It also gave us a chance to comment on each other's depiction of themselves and our sense of their strengths and weaknesses."

**Second question:** What does your soul look like? Draw a picture if that's easier than words.

**Example:** "This is a bit more difficult," says Gillian. "It needs to be clear that you may or may not feel you have a soul, but it gives people a chance to speak up about their spiritual beliefs. They talk about their connection with the universe and their dreams of how they want to make a difference."

### Variation

Have staff members sit across from each other. The exercise has me draw you as I believe your higher self—your angel—would see you. You do the same for me. This allows you to share what's glowing and emerging from the other person.

## Summary: Facilitate Personal Growth

This chapter introduced the importance of defining your business as a vehicle for personal and organizational transformation. As you focus on helping people grow, you will change as well. In fact, personal inner work often precedes organizational changes.

Change is best motivated by joy and hope, not fear and crisis, though change is always uncomfortable. Part of a leader's job is to push people by appealing not to their consciences but to their *greatness*. In particular, the power of stories helps create a picture of a better future that you can connect to their hopes and dreams. A leader nurtures inward toward intimacy as much as outward toward the market.

Values-based leaders view the purpose of business differently than do others. They look not only inward toward personal growth but also outside their company for ways to help transform the quality of life for all. The leadership of Judy Wicks exemplified an interest in growing sustainable local communities of people in positive relationships above growing the sales of her own company. In the next chapter, we'll examine the final leadership practice: collaborating for greater impact. It focuses on how to go beyond traditional company borders to increase your social and financial impact.

# 7

## Collaborate for Greater Impact

> Leadership styles evolve. There's always the vision-
> ary role to some extent, but inspiring and envision-
> ing gets old. Influencing, cajoling, and collaborating
> are more sustainable. Great values-based leaders
> are colearners. They're not mentors but more bi-
> directional *nurturers*. Nurturing the genius in others
> is how to be most effective. For most leaders, it's a
> huge learning process to move from hierarchy to
> collaboration, and for some, it's impossible.
>
> TOM REIS, PROGRAM DIRECTOR, PHILANTHROPY AND
> VOLUNTEERISM, W. K. KELLOGG FOUNDATION

The fifth and final stage in the process of leading a best-in-class values-based small business is collaborating for greater impact. We'll look at some common myths and examples of the practice of collaboration beyond your company's borders that will increase your ability to create a world that reflects your values.

### Why Is It Important to Collaborate for Greater Impact?

The practice of collaboration within a company has been well documented over the past twenty years. Similarly, the ins and outs of successful mergers and acquisitions have received much attention. This discussion, however, is about the spirit of Tom Reis's advice taken a step further to include stakeholders beyond employees and beyond the traditional boundaries of a company. A good previous example is Judy Wicks, who "collaborates" with competitors to increase the demand for free-range pork in Philadelphia.

Tom's advice requires leaders to collaborate inside and outside their companies. If you don't develop a collaborative culture within the company, you're not going to be a good collaborator outside the company. The culture you develop in your business must reflect and honor the value of collaboration. That changes your job as its leader. You need to be *more of a diplomat, less of a dictator.*

I've been impressed by how values-based leaders are redefining "compassion," how they're increasing their effectiveness by focusing on inner emotional and spiritual work as the keys to organizational transformation and greater social impact. But the dominant theme today is the desire of values-based leaders to make an impact greater than they can attain by simply developing a solitary company. As many admit, no matter how big they grow their companies, they can do only so much. So they've started to look for other leaders and companies to partner with to leverage their ability to change the world.

For example, since 1978, former SVN board chair Ed Dugger has been the president and CEO of UNC Partners (formerly Urban National Corporation), whose private venture capital funds support entrepreneurs of color. Through UNC, Ed has leveraged more than $2 billion in financing for minority-owned businesses. Still, he recognizes that his mission to bring entrepreneurs of color into the business mainstream is a "huge undertaking that goes far beyond UNC or any resources I can muster."

Ed has spent his career demonstrating the success and sound economics of these ventures, asking himself, how do you make black capitalism a respectable endeavor? His reply: "We need success stories. I can support black enterprises by sitting on their boards, creating networks to connect us with business leaders of major corporations, and, of course, by continuing to make capital available."

To do this, Ed developed a collaborative leadership style. In the late 1970s, he began hiring African-American interns from Harvard Business School to give them exposure to an industry that had not previously been available to minorities. He took them on deal negotiations and gave them opportunities to be involved that are rarely experienced by summer interns, all of whom he partnered with and nurtured. Today, many of Ed's UNC disciples have moved into top finance positions, furthering the UNC mission.

Strong in diplomatic skills, Ed helped launch the Business Collaborative, a nonprofit business membership group of major corporate leaders and entrepreneurs of color. His board position at the Federal Reserve Bank of Boston gave him access to major corporate CEOs who joined the group. His biggest surprise: "A number of CEOs whom I never thought of asking for support have been tremendously helpful once I asked. You need to be careful making assumptions about who can be valuable collaborators," Ed points out, reaffirming Van Woods's lesson in the previous chapter.

In April 2005, the Business Collaborative spawned the *Initiative for a New Economy* to expand commerce between local minority-owned businesses and large corporations. Seed funding totaling $1.3 million was provided by a unique local collaboration that included the City of Boston, Blue Cross Blue Shield of Massachusetts, Liberty Mutual, the Boston Foundation, and the United Way of Mass Bay.

Sitting on several black enterprise boards, Ed reflects on his mission: "Today, businesses of color are the fastest growing segment in numbers in the economy. What was a social responsibility issue is now an economic issue. We need to help the leaders grow their companies. That will take a different mentality and a change in corporate culture to fit this new group of young leaders." It's a mission worthy of further collaboration.

## Myth 1: Establish Your Business First and Then Collaborate.

### Truth 1: Collaboration Can Be Your Business from the Start

Collaboration can be a natural maturation process. Once your company gets to a certain size, you think of new ways to have an impact. But as a values-based small business leader, why not go outside your company to maximize your impact as early as possible? Often, it's because you're afraid that if you focus too much on collaboration, you'll lose sight of your core business. You feel you have enough to do and your company is not stable enough yet. Collaboration also requires additional personal skills. But in many cases, when you rethink your role and your business, collaboration is at the core of your "new" business and how you build your position in the marketplace. Just make sure your mission is big enough!

"My mission is to reduce carbon output in the world," says venture capitalist and social entrepreneur Artemis Joukowsky. In 1989, Artemis cofounded Highland Energy Group, a national energy services company that produced $50 million in energy-efficiency projects for large energy consumers. Its success led to its sale in 1997 to a subsidiary of Eastern Utility Associates, a $2 billion NYSE company at that time.

Since 1999, Artemis has been vice chairman of Ecoenergy International, an industry leader in greenhouse gas management services and in emission reduction purchase programs. His company collaborates with energy producers, corporations, financial institutions, governments, and NGOs (nongovernmental organizations) to find practical, cost-effective ways to implement clean and efficient energy solutions globally. What exactly does Artemis do?

"It took 15 years for Tom [Stoner, Artemis's longtime business partner] and I to develop the track record and the relationships we needed to build these alternative energy companies. The keys are *focus* and *scale*. I'm focused on what to do to build the business. That means I'm always looking for how to take it to scale."

For example, at Ecoenergy, Artemis and Tom found a small Boulder, Colorado, company that had been handling $30,000–$50,000 energy projects for the past ten years. They asked, "If they can execute at those sizes, what will it take to do $30–$50 million projects?" In 2005, the company was working on nearly $1 billion worth of energy projects in five countries on two continents.

What it takes is collaboration, something the physically challenged Artemis has done his whole life. It has made him think differently from others about how he lives his life and how he does business: "I've learned to reframe the energy service business by collaborating. I first look for a partner who's done this kind of work before at bigger levels, then a partner who's willing to take on the financing risks, and finally a long-term financial partner who has strategic and political interest in that project."

Today, Ecoenergy collaborates in emerging markets with banks like the World Bank and its Inter-American Bank to finance projects in China and Latin America. Artemis's work is to reshape the company: "We repositioned Ecoenergy from a consulting company to a venture fund. It's something we're good at. It makes us a good partner for our partners."

Big dreams and big missions usually require big organizations and many employees to fulfill those dreams and missions. Rather than trying to captain a large company, however, you may find it easier to build a small company that will be a good partner for others who can help you have the impact of a much larger company. To do so, you will need to position your company differently (e.g., as a venture fund, not a consulting company), focusing on a very specialized skill. Your job will change, too; you'll spend more time outside your company as a diplomat with less organizational hierarchy internally.

## Myth 2: Collaboration Does Not Appreciably Affect Your Role.

### Truth 2: Collaboration Requires Leadership without Control

Most values-based leaders wait too long to give up control of parts of their jobs. If you're used to operating your company as a partnership, relinquishing control is much easier. I'm not, and I know I have trouble letting go. This founder's curse makes it difficult to successfully collaborate. However, ways do exist to give up control and keep control of what's important. Look at how "eco-preneurs" Sylvie Blanchet and Thomas Fricke do it.

In 1996, a question—How do we convince small-scale farmers in Sumatra not to encroach on the boundaries of the biologically important Kerinci Seblat Park Preserve?—led to the founding of ForesTrade, the world's leading supplier of organic and sustainably produced tropical spices, vanilla, essential oils, and fair-trade coffee. The $10.4 million company (2004) directly sources products from over 5,000 small-scale, indigenous farmers in Indonesia and Guatemala.

Sylvie and Thomas credit their rapid success in large part to a number of innovative partnerships and alliances, which include producers, processors, NGOs, investors, financial institutions, and customers around the world. What makes the extensive collaborations work? They look for partners who share similar values and, therefore, are willing to abide by certain rules. They also compensate them financially for following certain restrictions on where and how their land is farmed.

ForesTrade was established to serve as a vehicle for sustainable agriculture and sustainable development and to protect sensitive ecosystems through a for-profit enterprise. For protecting resources and supporting conservation, farmers receive a direct price incentive and access to affordable credit. ForesTrade requires the farmers to practice shade cultivation and organic production, to keep reserves protected from development on the farm where appropriate, and not to hunt endangered species.

"We want to have a positive influence on these communities, and it's important that we're profitable," says Sylvie. "To keep the integrity of our values throughout the entire supply chain requires more of our time and effort away from home to monitor. Monitoring the proper implementation of these ecological values can be very taxing and complex due to the traveling and language barriers. But in the end, we know we're making a difference for all of our organizations and for the planet."

Sylvie and Thomas have created a business through collaboration by directly compensating and monitoring partners to keep their mission and values intact. Joel Solomon provides another practical way to collaborate without control.

As president of Renewal Partners and executive director of the Endswell Foundation, Joel's mission is to utilize early-stage investing and charitable grant making to promote a sustainable, environmentally beneficial vision for the British Columbia economy. Investor Solomon wears many hats, but ultimately, he's a *citizen*.

After inheriting $5 million on his father's death, Joel partnered with a fellow inheritor in 1992, Carol Newell, to focus their wealth on social change in British Columbia. Currently, he's directing his energies to the coast: "We have only 30,000 people on 21 million acres that are pretty much intact, and eleven First Nations indigenous tribes with no land treaties yet signed. Through venture and loan funds, grants for land use, and First Nations–owned business, we can cocreate a place where the environment, social justice, and sound economics live in harmony. It's a showpiece of what we've spent a decade developing."

To effect change and receive financial and nonfinancial returns, Joel must create connections among a myriad of businesses and government and community organizations. On the business side, for example, he supports emerging leaders with bridge financing and advice until they can attract other capital. He also brings in outside investors.

Joel works on the basis of a twenty-year plan: "In the first ten years, we were largely invisible. We built relationships between environmental, business, and indigenous groups. Now into our second decade, we must become more visible. We need to enter the public arena and politics and build values-based leadership there, too." Joel's emerging leaders have won three elections. One of these leaders is environmentalist Gregor Robertson, the CEO of Happy Planet, a fifty-person organic juice company Joel invested in, who was elected to the Provincial Legislature in 2004 to forward a values-based agenda.

The foundation of Joel's collaborative work stems from his principles and values, specifically regarding control and the moderation of financial returns to enhance social returns. "To keep some sanity on the planet," he holds three operating principles for collaboration:

1. *We are in only for the long term.* It takes time to build infrastructure.
2. *We collaborate with people who are or could be friends.* This means that we respect their motivations and values first, their business skills second, and their gift for making money third.

3. *We do not take control positions.* We want interdependence and we want our partners to have their own personalities.

With vision and values, with a quiet self-confidence and no need for control, Joel has constructed a collaborative network that's creating positive, sustainable change. He's done it profitably through a strong social portfolio and with a low-key leadership style and personality rarely seen among those of wealth and power.

## Myth 3: Values-Based Leaders Should Do Business Only with Values-Based Leaders.

### Truth 3: Keep Your Values Intact and Broaden Your Reach

Whether values-based leaders should do business only with values-based leaders is arguably the most controversial current topic for such leaders of established companies. This issue is important to think about early on, to discuss with staff and investors and set your standards. Not doing so can tear a company apart. I know. I was part of a four-person group that raised $13.5 million to launch our company on the NASDAQ. But we disagreed on whether to take money from a large investor as two members didn't like the investor's values. We had set no standards, didn't resolve our disagreement, tried to sweep it under the rug, and never made it onto the NASDAQ.

In contrast to my situation, we've discussed Seth Goldman selling his Honest Tea products in plastic containers at Target stores, Florence Sender negotiating for placement of her bath products also at Target, and Jane Hileman selling a piece of her company to Random House. They all had well-established values standards, they all educated staff and consumers on what they were doing and why, and they were all true to those values. They were also clear with all stakeholders about how these arrangements would work.

I'd now like to add the example of Gary Hirshberg of Stonyfield Farm. I chose Gary because his standing as a values-based leader is, in my opinion, of the highest level of integrity. In this instance, we're not talking about a formal partnership but a significant distribution deal nearly as powerful: Gary is negotiating to sell his organic yogurt through Wal-Mart. Is this the type of distribution a values-based leader should seek? If so, how do you do it? Gary's response is instructive: "The days of standing on principle unless you meet all my values are over because the planet and our species need solutions right now. I have something that Wal-Mart consumers want. Wal-Mart doesn't care what we do with our product as long as it turns on the shelves. Of course, we're not going to do anything that will take us away from our mission. We're in the organic agriculture business and want to grow the sales of organic products. By carrying our products, Wal-Mart may be more inclined to carry other organic products in the future.

"We want to sell to the mainstream. It doesn't mean we want our company to become 'mainstream.' We like stirring things up. Always did. Even when we were bushy tailed and naïve, we always wanted to change the way business is done, to show that you could keep your values and still be very profitable.

"Leadership can't be a frontal assault. It means first finding common ground. If you want to change the major companies— the big players in an industry—you have to at least be invited to sit at the table. The ultimate purpose is not necessarily to conquer and own my market. The mission is to get more farmland farmed ecologically so it can be sustained and get the toxins out of the atmosphere."

It's up to you as the leader to set the boundaries of your business deals and collaborations to preserve your mission but not to box your company into a corner of limited opportunities. Otherwise, as Gary says, "In the end, you become a rounding error" (i.e., so small in magnitude that your sales aren't worth including in calculating industry sales).

## Mistakes: What Kind of Collaborations Should You Be Careful to Avoid?

At the outset, let me be clear about some specific situations:

1. In raising capital, most leaders whose values are not aligned with the values of their investors have problems. (Don't fool yourself. I know of dozens of examples!)
2. In selecting business partners, refer to number one.
3. In hiring most kinds of employees, refer to number one.

Values, values, values. I can't tell you how many conversations I've had with values-based leaders about how they thought their values weren't important in a particular instance—"we really needed the money"—and their decisions came back to haunt them.

Two of my friends ran a well-known Southern California bagel company. With sales comfortably in the millions, they secured a long-term deal with a large national discount chain (not Wal-Mart). They expanded capacity. Sales climbed that year. The next year, the chain terminated the deal based on some fabricated excuse. My friends ended up selling the company for zilch.

The lesson was simple: *Be careful of collaborating with someone who has less to lose than you do if the partnership falls apart.* My friends had to build to capacity to get the contract, but the national chain was a low-cost, transactional concern. The

CEO was not known for anything but pursuing low cost. As Katie Paine (chapter 1) learned from growing a company with too much overhead and a high break-even volume, before launching a new company with less overhead, "Volume for the sake of overhead is lousy." That's where my friends put themselves with this deal.

Another example illustrates the importance of looking at collaborations from the potential partner's point of view. In the mid-1990s, SVN members who were manufacturers of supermarket products asked me to help with a "socially responsible" product section in national supermarkets. I'd spent years in that industry, had written two books, and had high-level connections.

I refused. Why would supermarkets want a "socially responsible" product section when it implied that the other 20,000 products they carried were socially *ir*responsible? Today, however, we have natural and organic sections that do imply that products in other sections are not natural or organic. And the supermarkets get great margins on those natural and organic products, too. This collaboration is in everyone's best interest.

Partnerships with nonprofit organizations require skill and *patience.* In my pet product business, we tried to make a deal with a national nonprofit group. We offered to put a message about its work on each of our products and give it 10 percent of our proceeds. Sounds simple. The problem was that since our products were often sold across state lines, we had to get fifty separate agreements from fifty local and state branches of the nonprofit. We chose another group.

*Collaborations work best when you initiate them but your staff runs them.* Having similar values and business cycles as the collaborative partner helps because you'll find more common ground for the rhythms of how you work together. The real key is that the partnership allows you each to do things you couldn't do without the other, with synergistic goals.

## Doing It Right: Collaborating to Build "Hybrid Value-Added Chains"

When you're a small business leader, everything is in short supply: funds, people, time, and information. That's why collaboration can be such a powerful boost. In particular, collaborating across business sectors is an opportunity small values-based business leaders should not overlook. Often a nonprofit organization has the market information and access to resources that may be unavailable to a for-profit company. With more of these partnerships occurring, they now have their own term.

Bill Drayton calls them "hybrid value-added chains," collaborative networks between the business and citizen sectors that create positive, sustainable, systemic change. That's a mouthful! But if you want to see the power of collaboration, there may be no better example. (Bill uses the terms "business sector" and "citizen sector." He feels that the "for-profit" and "nonprofit" distinctions are misleading.)

Bill is the founder and CEO of Ashoka, a global organization that scours the planet and invests in leading social entrepreneurs with the biggest ideas. Ashoka supports them with a stipend and its collaborative global network—*for life*. That's right, once you become an Ashoka fellow, it's for life, for as Bill emphasizes, "Change takes time."

Only Bill's unending dedication to Ashoka and its mission matches the patience required. Is it working? Since Ashoka began in 1980, it has supported 1,600 fellows in sixty countries. After five years, the average Ashoka fellow is serving 174,000 people!

If you ask Bill what his mission is, he'll tell you it's to "accelerate the emergence of an entrepreneurial citizen sector." But if you push him just a bit, he'll tell you that his real goal is to see a world in which *everyone is a change maker.* Ashoka fellows create large-scale structural changes: "We support entrepreneurs who will change dramatically the way things are done in their field on a continental scale. We link them with similarly skilled and dedicated people, like other Ashoka fellows, to carefully build community locally and globally."

The Ashoka fellows reframe a social challenge to find a solution. They bring together diverse groups to solve problems in everyone's best interest. In 2004, for example, Ashoka fellows started creating "hybrid value-added chains" of global partnerships between social entrepreneurs and business. Bill has found that as the citizen sector has become more entrepreneurial, it has become easier to marry the strengths of business with those of the citizen sector and create a more effective, efficient, collaborative chain of production and distribution that adds value for all concerned.

Ashoka not only sees the opportunity, but Bill, his staff, and fellows are able to persuade leading businesses and citizen groups to play these new collaborative roles. "The new pattern is so much more productive that business, the citizen sector, and the consuming public all are big winners," notes Bill.

For example, in Mexico, small farmers couldn't get irrigation equipment because distribution was too expensive for the piping company, which also didn't understand how local dynamics worked. So an Ashoka fellow found and introduced the piping company, Amanco, to small citizen groups that served and were trusted by the farmers. These groups had only recently developed the skills and scale to be cost-efficient partners with businesses. The result: the small farmers now have additional, more stable income and the water and environmental conservation benefits of drip irrigation; Amanco has large new markets and profits; and the citizen groups get a healthy markup with happy clients.

With arrangements like that accomplished, Ashoka and its fellows then leverage this innovative, value-adding chain around the world in other areas of need ranging from room additions to forestry. They collaborate with interested parties and encourage competition to spread these ideas so that consulting firms eventually take over Ashoka's initiating role.

From across the globe, Bill takes the "partial answers of these entrepreneurs and puts them together into 'mosaics': What are the universal principles here? What other ways can we merge the two sectors? Then we spread the innovation wherever it applies."

What can we learn from Bill about leading a collaborative operation for greater impact? First, entrepreneurs, like companies, grow most efficiently through collaboration with others. As Bill has observed, "We can do a lot more with two entrepreneurs working together than with two working alone. *Collaborative entrepreneurship* supports the development of the individual entrepreneur and spreads innovations more rapidly."

Second, selecting the right partners is critical. You can imagine the process of becoming a lifetime Ashoka fellow. Bill uses five criteria (what would be yours?):

1. Is this truly a transformational *new idea* for solving a social need?
2. Is this person *creative* in goal setting, overcoming obstacles, and seizing opportunities?
3. Is this person an *entrepreneur,* so committed that he or she won't rest until it happens?
4. Is the idea likely to have *social impact* at the national level and spread beyond?
5. Does the person have *ethical fiber*—a deep honesty and trustworthiness?

What does it take to lead a decentralized organizational structure with a myriad of relationships? Bill spent nine years at McKinsey consulting company and taught at Stanford Law

School and Harvard's Kennedy School of Government. He clearly has a flexible mind and the ability to be a politician or diplomat. He's creative, he's a deep thinker, and he's comfortable in many environments. Most important, *he has faith.* As Bill explains, "You have to when you're twenty-five years ahead of your time! We serve best as determined by history. With the citizen sector rapidly becoming more efficient, our field is now at a major inflection point, so we too must move fast right now to serve effectively [Ashoka's budget has grown 30–35 percent annually the past six years as funders have begun to agree with Bill's vision and support his collaborative methods]. This twenty-five-year trend of increased competency and scale may mean that it's finally time to bring the business and citizen sector together once and for all."

## How to Improve: Rethink Your Business

Growing a company can take you only so far. Values-based small business leaders look for ways to leverage their impact and build a stronger business. Collaboration requires you to acquire a new set of diplomatic skills and spend time outside your organization and industry. That will redefine the boundaries of your organization and give you a new role.

Here are five questions to ask yourself to help you collaborate more effectively:

1. *Do you know what it would take to have the social impact you desire?* What other organizations might increase your social impact? How do you balance short-term needs with long-term vision? Will the social impact of your collaboration also lead to a positive financial impact for your company?

2. *What is your role in collaborating with other organizations?* Is collaboration central to your organization's

financial success? How do you create the environment for your staff to become involved in collaborations? How do you establish competitive prices and policies with suppliers or distributors you wish to help?

3. *How do you improve your abilities and opportunities to collaborate?* Do you lead collaboratively or competitively or both? What can you do to move outside your organization and meet potential partners whom you don't meet in normal daily interactions? Do you lead collaborative relationships as you lead in your company?

4. *How will you keep collaborations on track and dissolve them if they are not working?* How will you measure the success of a collaboration? How much time will you devote to forming and monitoring these alliances? What will you not do to gain time for collaborative efforts?

5. *How might collaboration redefine your organization and the business you are in?* Do you see your organization as part of a system instead of a member of an industry? How do you distinguish becoming an educational advocacy group from offering a business service? How does any redefinition change your role?

## Action Exercise: Thinking Outside the Industry

This exercise returns us to the section in chapter 1 on leading a responsible company. It's an exercise I use with executives and company founders to help them look at the purpose of their life's work. The goal is to broaden your thinking on what kinds of leaders and companies may be good collaborators for you as you build a business that reflects your values.

Sit down with your staff and map out possible alliances that you feel would strengthen your financial results and your social and environmental mission. Some alliances will do one or the other; some may strengthen both. Try to think creatively of competitors, other industries, other organizational forms, individuals, and political and citizen groups.

Start by rephrasing the questions from "Leading Responsibility: Is Altruism in Your Best Interest?" in chapter 1:

1. What is the dominant social issue of your mission?
2. What do you need to do to have an impact on this issue?
3. What alliances would help you meet that challenge?

You will use a method similar to chapter 4's three-step process of walking toward the talk. A good starting point is to answer the questions in the previous section, particularly question five. Please also use your responses to the action exercises on translating values into value and walking toward the talk here. To illustrate parts of the analysis, I will use my writing business as an example. I write books and, since March 1996, a monthly e-newsletter ($50 per year fee) that serves subscribers in eighty-seven countries.

**Step 1.** *Make a general assessment of the three questions.* Make two columns on a sheet of paper, one for "Social Impact" and one for "Financial Impact." Down the left side of these columns, make three rows corresponding to the three questions above: "Issue," "Requirements," and "Alliances." Fill in the first column, drawing on your past exercises and the questions in the previous section to help you rethink your business and its boundaries.

**Example:** The dominant social issue of my writing business is how to humanize the way we do business so that it uplifts the human spirit and helps alleviate poverty and suffering on our planet. What is required is to help businesspeople find their own way to make a difference in the world, make good livings, and have fulfilling personal lives. Helpful alliances outside my industry include career counselors and coaches, organizational consulting companies, foundations focused on leadership and social entrepreneurship, and company human resource strategy and training departments. (Within the industry, spiritual/self-help speakers, writers, and Web sites are some of the more obvious alliance candidates.)

**Step 2.** *Assess the financial impact of the information from step 1.* Fill in the second column, "Financial Impact," with the key financial issues corresponding to the responses you wrote in the first column. For example, will you need to raise money to support your social mission at the outset? Could a certain alliance minimize your overhead? Use all the space you need, which may include extra pages, but try to be specific.

**Example:** Briefly, the social focus of my mission asks readers to extend themselves to others. As they are not benefiting financially from me, at least not directly, they are not inclined to support me financially to any great extent, either. In addition, many readers are out of work or soon will be, and my work often directs them into work and lifestyle changes that will decrease their income in the near term. The financial implications are that I need to keep costs low, raise capital, and increase revenues through alliances.

**Step 3.** *Prioritize potential alliances.* On a separate sheet of paper, give yourself two sets of 100 points to allocate among potential alliances in terms of their importance for your company's social mission and financial health. These two sets of numbers usually differ. Meet with staff on Monday morning to reconcile the differences and develop a plan for how you will proceed to build these alliances.

**Example:** For the social mission, I allocated the 100 points as follows: career counselors and coaches, 50 points; organizational consulting companies, 10; foundations focused on leadership and social entrepreneurship, 20; and company human resource strategy and training departments, 20. For the financial impact, I allocated the 100 points as follows: career counselors and coaches, 15 points; organizational consulting companies, 20; foundations focused on leadership and social entrepreneurship, 15; and company human resource strategy and training departments, 50. And I'm still planning!

## Summary: Collaborate for Greater Impact

This chapter introduced the importance of defining your business more broadly as part of a collaborative system to increase its social and financial impact. As a values-based business leader, your focus should be on thinking outside traditional company boundaries and developing the diplomatic and relational skills to chose the right values-based partners.

Collaboration can be a key element from the start in building a business that reflects your values. Part of your personal development requires you to be comfortable operating with less control than you are used to exercising. To adjust to having less control, you should set down clear values standards for collaboration. A key issue is whether or not and how to deal with leaders who don't express similar values.

Bill Drayton and Ashoka are an example of how you can create effective, efficient social change on a large scale through collaboration with a diverse group of partners. It requires creative thinking, a network of like-minded organizations, and a dedication and patience to work out new ways to deliver products and services. In the final chapter, let's consider the challenges of values-based leadership and the most effective ways to build a business that reflects your values.

# Leadership Is Learning

When you go to the office next Monday morning, *what are you going to do differently?* That's my question for you.

Learning is valuable, but *impact* is what this book is all about. That comes from helping you change the way you lead and how you impact others through your business.

Leadership is an act of liberation, not of control. It starts with liberating yourself and finding your way. Paradoxically, that will happen only when you help others reach *their* full potential and discover their greatness—when you inspire them to dream more, do more, and be more.

These were certainly not my concerns when I started a business to reflect my values. Yes, I wanted to be true to myself, but I wasn't much worried about anyone else. Business is difficult enough without worrying about everyone else. I'd left a good job and had enough to deal with as my business floundered at the start. I needed more sales and stronger finance, I thought. Then, slowly I realized that what I really needed were people who were as committed as I was to making this business work.

That's when I started thinking about values in terms of a mission bigger than all of us that would get all of us excited.

Such a mission meant that I had a lot to learn about leadership and more still about values-based leadership. It meant that I had to think differently about what I did and how I spent my time. It meant that I had to focus on people as much as products, process as much as productivity, and principles as much as profits.

This book distills what I've learned over the past two decades from my experiences and those of other values-based leaders. I learned from making mistakes, recovering from those mistakes, questioning myself, and ultimately finding myself by making a difference in the lives of people in my company and beyond.

I hope that reading this book has shifted something inside you. I hope that it can support you on the tough but tremendously fulfilling journey of values-based leadership. To that end, let me recap what I see as five practical themes of the book.

## Make Values Visible

Founder of *Ms.* magazine Gloria Steinem says that you can tell what your values are by looking at your checkbook stubs. Whatever you decide are your values, arguably your most important job is to make them visible through your actions and words— and yes, Ms. Steinem, through how you deploy your company's financial assets.

Live these values in everything you do. It's one of the great advantages of having you, the founder, around. If values are going to serve as a corporate asset to help grow your company rather than as a corporate liability that seemingly complicates every decision, your every interaction should embody those values.

Consider your business conversations and the conversations at your company. How do you converse and what's the focus of these conversations? Your answers to those questions are your values. You're the walking, breathing symbol of what the company stands for. Act on your values and be clear about their boundaries, especially when challenged by business realities.

The CEO of Original Artists and the only woman to win a Grammy as the producer of the Song of the Year ("Don't Worry, Be Happy"), Linda Goldstein, represents performers whose "creativity I translate into bottom-line realities." She deals in an industry that's all about money, "yet the heart and soul of what it takes to be an artist has nothing to do with that. I develop the strategic partnerships where the best deals often translate into the ones that require the least paperwork."

Don't forget that while words are nice, what really matters is how you act. Don't obsess about how your values and mission are spelled out. Most companies use similar words yet translate them into very different behaviors.

As a resource, check out "The Value of Corporate Values" in the Summer 2005 issue of *Strategy & Business* a survey on values of 9,500 senior executives from around the world by consultant Booz Allen and the Aspen Institute think tank. The article is also available at the *Strategy & Business* Web site.

## Make It Personal

Business is about building relationships. Relationships are personal. Be personal. Bring all of yourself to work and expect others to do so, too. Most important, as Calvert Group CEO Barbara Krumsiek made clear, make sure you continue to communicate individually and personally as much as possible.

Often as companies grow, leaders start efficiency campaigns. They limit personal interaction and no longer tailor their communications to the needs of different individuals. If Barbara can remain personal with 200 employees, you can do it in your organization! This tends to become a major challenge at around fifty people. That's when it becomes difficult to know everyone personally. In reality, however, this issue is about how you decide to spend your time and how you honor the importance of personal growth, not just sales growth.

There is no substitute for personal interaction. Rather than spending your time dreaming up strategy by yourself or with a few key people, consider coming down from your mountaintop and increasing your face time with your staff. Don't listen to those who tell you that with a bigger company you need to be more "professional" or "efficient." A minute of personal interaction does wonders for making strategy happen.

## Communicate Clearly, Consistently, and Simply

Leadership is about what happens when you're not there. Your communication needs to be so clear and simple that those you're with can relay exactly what you said to others when you're not around.

Be mindful that people will interpret everything you do. And when you talk with one person, before you know it everyone in the company will have heard what you said. If you're not clear and simple, your message may be changed into something different from what you intended. Clarity and simplicity are also important for selling your ideas.

For example, the president of the Youth Empowerment Alliance, Sherry Sacino, wrote *Keeping the Drive Alive* in 1995 and *Spiritual Touchdowns* in 1998, selling over 400,000 copies. She got substantial help from the NFL (National Football League) and the players' union, not an easy task. What Sherry did well was communicate what she wanted to do so clearly, so simply, that whomever she told of her project could easily repeat it to others.

"I want to write a book of brief, uplifting, life-defining stories of NFL players to be distributed to children," she told Sam Wyche, head coach of the NFL's Tampa Bay Buccaneers from 1992 to 1995. Sam conveyed the one-liner to his team, they sent out a letter to raise money to publish the first book, Sam talked to the NFL, and Sherry was on her way. The second book required little more than a few phone calls to the same people.

## Let Go of Control but Stay Involved

As they grow and mature, companies typically develop love-hate relationships with their founders—not unlike teenagers and their parents. On the one hand, the company has needed its leader so desperately to survive and grow. On the other hand, people feel they can do things themselves and often the leader just gets in the way.

Giving up control and letting your company "grow up" is hard. But if you don't let go, not only will you slow the healthy growth of your company and staff, but you'll also burn out. The trick is knowing when to let go and what to let go of to do it in a way that keeps you involved enough just to make sure things don't get out of hand. Remember that you are the designer, the architect of your company, not the "ship's captain." Your job is to create the right environment and then step away.

For example, don't give up control of the checkbook. Cash flow is the name of the game. You need to stay on top of that as those numbers tell you a lot about your business. Also, stay as involved as possible with decisions about people. This is less important for product-related decisions, unless that's something you enjoy.

General Electric is famous for its CEO succession. Your first day as CEO of General Electric is the day you begin to look for and then groom your replacement. For small business leaders, I would alter that a bit. The day you establish the company should be the day you start looking for a COO, a chief operating officer; a CEO comes later. The "when" to let go is almost always sooner than you think, but not until cultural values are in place. Gary Erickson of Clif Bar pointed out that when he turned over the CEO job to Sheryl O'Loughlin in 2004, he did have clear, visible values criteria in place. Sheryl knew that making a product mistake was forgivable but not a values mistake. That's how the strong culture and explicit values Gary instilled in the company have taken over the control he once had.

## Be Careful of Two Double-Edged Swords: Compassion and Responsibility

If I'm asked what's the most common mistake made by values-based leaders, this is my answer. You may be too slow to fire, too "nice" to challenge people, or too hesitant to face tough internal decisions when business slows. You may be so generous with employee benefits, so focused on making a social contribution, or so easy on small suppliers or collaborators that you forget you're in business.

Values-based leadership is about not accepting an "or" but looking for the "and." By this I mean looking for ways to do something that will have a good financial impact *and* a good social impact. Sometimes that's easy to do, but sometimes it isn't possible. Keep trying but develop a culture that understands this and makes decisions in a way that supports the intention of your values and your financial integrity.

Values-based leaders are often too hard on themselves. Be proud of the fact that you're *trying* to incorporate social objectives into your business. Be proud of the fact that social contribution is part of daily conversations at your company. Be proud of the fact that you're focused on your employees as whole people more than as profit machines.

The truth is, you can't always do it all. Compassion and responsibility are virtues that we strive for, but if you don't run a financially strong business, people will be out of work. Not rooting out people who don't fit with your culture will negatively impact those who do fit. Be clear on what you mean and don't mean by "compassion" and "responsibility."

## In Conclusion

Values-based leaders need lots of patience, faith, and courage: the patience required to build something that has multiple objectives beyond profitability, the faith that those intangibles of company culture and social and environmental contribution really are as important as the very tangible sales and profit, and the courage to trust that the universe takes care of those who reach for their dreams. As a values-based leader, you need the sense of purpose you get from knowing that you're doing something you were meant to do.

I'm often asked why I do what I do. Ask yourself the same question. Why are you a values-based leader? I think your answers are quite similar to mine. It's the path you've chosen to fulfill your destiny, the lifelong journey of finding out how to be true to yourself. I wish you Godspeed.

# Resources

Of the seventy-five Social Venture Network leaders interviewed, material from sixty-six was included in the book. Their company names and Web site or e-mail contacts as well as other helpful resources are listed below if you're interested in further information.

Carol Atwood, Spartacus Media Enterprises,
http://www.spartacusmedia.net/smeHome.htm
Kenny Ausubel, Bioneers/Collective Heritage Institute,
http://www.bioneers.org
Joan Bavaria, Trillium Asset Management,
http://www.trilliuminvest.com
David Berge, Underdog Ventures, LLC,
http://www.underdogventures.com
Scott Blackwell, Immaculate Baking Co.,
http://www.immaculatebaking.com
Sylvie Blanchet and Thomas Fricke, ForesTrade, Inc.,
http://www.forestrade.com
Melissa Bradley, New Capitalist and Reentry Strategies Institute,
http://www.newcapitalist.com
Adrienne Maree Brown, League of Pissed Off Voters,
adrienne@indyvoter.org
Gillian Caldwell, WITNESS,
http://www.witness.org
Allan Cohen, Babson College,
http://www3.babson.edu
Gun Denhart, Hanna Andersson Children's Foundation,
http://www.hannafoundation.org
Amy Domini, Domini Social Investments, LLC,
http://www.domini.com

Bill Drayton, Ashoka: Innovators for the Public,
  http://www.ashoka.org
Geralyn White Dreyfous, Salt Lake City Film Center,
  http://www.slcfilmcenter.org
Ed Dugger, UNC Partners, Inc.,
  http://www.uncpartners.com
Adnan Durrani, Condor Ventures, Inc., and Blue Chip Venture
  Company,
  http://www.bcvc.com
Gary Erickson, Clif Bar, Inc.,
  http://www.clifbar.com
Mark A. Finser, RSF,
  http://www.rsfsocialfinance.org
Eric Friedenwald-Fishman, Metropolitan Group,
  http://www.metgroup.com
Jay Coen Gilbert, AND 1,
  jcoengilbert@comcast.net
Seth Goldman, Honest Tea,
  http://www.honesttea.com
Linda Goldstein, Original Artists,
  Linda@originalartists.com
Alisa Gravitz, Co-op America,
  http://www.coopamerica.org
Danny Grossman, Wild Planet Toys, Inc.,
  http://www.wildplanet.com
Joyce Haboucha. Rockefeller & Co., Inc.,
  http://www.rockco.com
Laury Hammel, Longfellow Clubs,
  http://longfellowclubs.com
Darrell Hammond, KaBOOM!,
  http://www.kaboom.org
Lori Hanau, Global Roundtable Leadership,
  lorihanau@verizon.net
Jane Hileman, American Reading Company,
  http://www.americanreading.com
Gary Hirshberg, Stonyfield Farm, Inc.,
  http://www.stonyfield.com

Elliot Hoffman, Just Desserts and New Voice of Business,
elliothoffman@sbcglobal.net
Jeffrey Hollender, Seventh Generation,
http://www.seventhgeneration.com
Artemis Joukowsky, Avalon Financial Group and Ecoenergy
International,
http://www.econergy.net
Judith Katz, The Kaleel Jamison Consulting Group, Inc.,
http://www.kjcg.com
Jim Kelly, Rejuvenation, Inc.,
http://www.rejuvenation.com
Barbara Krumsiek, Calvert Group, Ltd.,
http://www.calvert.com
Marc Lesser, ZBA Associates,
http://www.zbaassociates.com
Josh Mailman, Mailman Foundation,
siriusb@pipeline.com
Steve Mariotti, National Foundation for Teaching
Entrepreneurship,
http://www.nfte.com
Linda Mason, Bright Horizons Family Solutions,
http://www.brighthorizons.com
Terry Mollner, Trusteeship Institute, Inc.,
terry@trusteeship.org
Deb Nelson and Pamela Chaloult, Social Venture Network,
http://www.svn.org
Katie Paine, KDPaine & Partners,
http://www.measuresofsuccess.com
Steve Piersanti, Berrett-Koehler Publishers,
http://www.bkconnection.com
Gifford Pinchot, Bainbridge Graduate Institute,
http://www.bgiedu.org
Bart Potenza and Joy Pierson, Candle Cafe,
http://www.candlecafe.com
Will Raap, Gardener's Supply Company,
http://www.gardeners.com
Tom Reis, W. K. Kellogg Foundation,
http://www.wkkf.org

Sherry Sacino, Youth Empowerment Alliance, Inc.,
http://www.yealliance.org
Florence Sender, FoodLogic, LCC,
florence@styr.com
Joe Sibilia, Meadowbrook Capital
http://www.meadowbrooklane.com
Wayne Silby, Calvert Group, Ltd.,
http://www.calvert.com
Tami Simon, Sounds True Inc.,
http://www.soundstrue.com
Nina Simons, Bioneers/Collective Heritage Institute,
http://www.bioneers.org
Joel Solomon, Renewal Partners and the Endswell Foundation,
http://www.renewalpartners.com
Greg Steltenpohl, Odwalla and Adina for Life, Inc.,
http://www.adinaworld.com
Woody Tasch, Investors' Circle,
http://www.investorscircle.net
Hal Taussig, Idyll, Ltd., and Untours,
http://www.untours.com
Nina Utne, *Utne* Magazine,
http://www.utne.com
Julius Walls, Greyston Bakery,
http://www.greystonbakery.com
Mal Warwick, Mal Warwick & Associates, Inc.,
http://www.malwarwick.com
Judy Wicks, White Dog Cafe,
http://www.whitedog.com
Van Woods, Sylvia Woods Enterprises, LLC,
http://www.sylviassoulfood.com

# Index

compassion, 40–46, 54, 109–110, 132, 156–157
competence, 35–40, 54
competencies of founders, 35
conflict(s), 2, 97
connecting to yourself, 67–68
consistency, 107
control
    leadership without, 136–139
    letting go of, 36, 75, 85–86, 155–156
    losing/maintaining, 47–48
conversations, 152–153
Co-op America, 100–101
corporate social responsibility, 50
Corporate Social Responsibility (Natural Marketing Institute), 29
courtesy, 102–103
Crawford, Kit, 48
crisis as motivator of transformation, 116–117
cruelty-free initiatives, 124–125
culture. See also mission
    behavior and respect, 76
    building, 75–77
    cultural correction program, 31
    democratic, 42
    difficulty of building, 90
    keeping values on track with, 86
    questions for leading, 86
    Sounds True's, 66
    values-based versus leadership-driven, 77–78

daily meaning, 82–85
Davis, Julia, 94
deaf employees, 100–101
decision making, 2, 43, 87–90
    for strategic focus, 13–15
defining your business, 127
Denhart, Gun, 43–44
determinants of financial success, 14
diplomacy versus dictatorship, 132
disagreements, 95
disempowerment, 35
diversity, 101, 127–128
Domini, Amy, 50, 103–104
Domini 400 Social Index, 50
doubt, power of, 16–17
Drayton, Bill, 143, 150
Dreyfous, Geralyn White, 116

Dugger, Ed, 132–134
Durrani, Adnan, 20–21, 23

Ecoenergy International, 134–135
educational experience, 60
effectiveness, 95–97, 146–147
Eileen Fisher Company, 27. See also Fisher, Eileen
emotions, engaging, 58
empathy, 41, 109–110
employees
    CEOs' involvement with, 75–77, 86
    compassionate treatment of, 43–44
    deaf, 100–101
    ESOPs (employee stock ownership plans), 85, 126
    firing, 30–31
    involvement with, 155–156
    layoffs, 41–42, 84
    mission and values for, 74
    responsibilities to, 127
    right number of, 24
    supporting, 96–97
enthusiasm, 116
entrepreneurship, collaborative, 145–146
environment, providing fulfilling, 86
environmental responsibility, 14
Erickson, Gary, 48, 61, 156
ESOPs (employee stock ownership plans), 85, 126
ethos, 109
exit strategies, 47

facilitating personal growth. See growth
fear as motivator of transformation, 116–117
feedback, 98
fierce conversations model, 97–98
financial impact of alliances, 149–150
financial success
    commitment for, 51–53
    determinants of, 14
finding your place, 26
Finser, Mark A., 104–106, 110
First Nations, 137–139
Fisher, Eileen, 21, 27
FoodLogic, 38–40
ForesTrade, 136–137
founders, 35, 83, 136

principles, standing on, 140–141
Procter & Gamble, 50
productivity, 19
profit sharing, 84–85

qualities for values-based leaders, 157
  CEOs, 47
  commitment, 46–53, 54
  compassion, 40–46, 54
  competence, 35–40, 54
  overview, 33–34
quality of communication, 154–155
questions
  for effective collaboration, 146–
    147
  for opening communication, 108
  turning values into value, 67–68

Raap, Will, 22–23
Random House, 53
Reis, Tom, 131–132
Rejuvenation, 30–31, 76
relationships
  building personal, 153–154
  loving, 44–46
  with other businesses, 27
  transforming, 128–129
Renewal Partners, 137–139
respectful treatment, 43
responsibility
  compassion/responsibility-related
    mistakes, 156–157
  *Corporate Social Responsibility*
    (Natural Marketing Institute),
    29
  to employees, 127
  environmental, 14
  industry, 27–29
  social, 24–31, 50
Robertson, Gregor, 138
Robinson, Larry, 95
Robinson Jewelers, 95
Roddick, Anita, 5–6
roles
  CEOs', myths/truths about, 75–79
  collaboration-related, 136–139,
    146–147
  identifying your, 89–90

Rudolf Steiner Foundation (RSF),
  104–106
Rysavy, Jirka, 65

Sacino, Sherry, 154–155
sales as goal, 77–78
Save the Children, 60, 98
secrets, 15. *See also* transparency
self-actualization, 58
self-connection, 67–68
Sender, Florence, 38–40, 139
sensitivity, increasing your, 106–107
service experience, 59–60
Sibilia, Joe, 30
Silby, Wayne, 3, 78
Simon, Tami, 64–67, 71
Simons, Nina, 16–17
skills, key leadership, 59
social issues, identifying, 148–149
social responsibility, leading, 24–31
Social Venture Network (SVN), 3–4,
  33–34, 60, 83, 113–116, 169
societal impact of values-based leadership, 79
Solomon, Joel, 137–139
Sounds True, 64–67, 71
speaking ability, 99–101
*Spiritual Touchdowns* (Sacino), 154
*Sports Illustrated,* 80–82
SROI (social return index), 118
stakeholders, 79
Steinem, Gloria, 152
Steltenpohl, Greg, 77
stockholders, 117
stock valuation, predictors of, 78
Stoner, Tom, 135
Stonyfield Farm, 61–62, 140
stories, evoking joy and hope through,
  116–117
strategic focus, deciding on, 13–15
*Strategy & Business* magazine, 153
stress, reducing, 28
surveys, company mindfulness of environment, 29
sustainability, 15, 19–24, 31–32, 41
Sylvia's Restaurant, 121–123

Target, 39
Tasch, Woody, 8–9

team building, 77, 78
The Merchandising Group (TMG),
    28–29
thinking, challenging conventional, 126
three-dimensional thinking, 108
*Time* magazine, 51
time management, 107
TMG (The Merchandising Group),
    28–29
transformation. *See* organizational
    transformation
transparency, 15–19, 18–19, 31
Trillium Asset Management, 17–18
truth, 97–99. *See also* myths and truths
two-dimensional thinking, 108

UNC Partners, 132–133
Underdog Ventures, 58–59
Unilever, 107
Utne, Eric, 61
Utne, Nina, 61
*Utne* magazine, 61

value-added chains, hybrid, 143–146
"Value of Corporate Values" (*Strategy
    & Business*), 153
values
    business-to-business issues of, 139–
        141
    collaboration issues and, 141–142
    embedment in products/services, 80
    evolution of, 60–62
    importance of boundaries for, 37–
        40
    migrating toward, 62

values, *continued*
    myths/truths about, 58–62
    personal, 57–58, 64–67
    sacredness of your, 63–64
    translating, into company culture,
        86
    visibility of, 152–153
values-based business movement, 6
values-based leadership
    challenge of, 1–3
    definition of, 2–3
    qualities of, 157
values-to-value
    personal inventory creation, 68–70
    process, 58–59, 67–68, 70–71
    vendors, treatment of, 44–45
vision, company, losing, 81–82
volume, 24

walking toward the talk, 73–75. *See
    also* launching a company
Walls, Julius, 112, 124
Wal-Mart, 140
Warwick, Mal, 82–85, 90–91
Welch, Jack, 14
White Dog Cafe, 124–126
Wicks, Judy, 124–126, 131–132
Wild Planet Toys, 16, 27, 48, 60
WITNESS, 128
women in leadership positions, 16–17
Woods, Sylvia, 121–123
Woods, Van, 121–124
Wyche, Sam, 155

Ziegler, Mel, 113

# About Social Venture Network

SVN transforms the way the world does business by connecting, leveraging, and promoting a global community of leaders for a more just and sustainable economy. Since its founding in 1987, SVN has grown from a handful of visionary individuals into a vibrant community of 400 business owners, investors, and nonprofit leaders who are advancing the movement for social responsibility in business. SVN members believe in a new bottom line for business, one that values healthy communities and the human spirit as well as high returns.

As a network, SVN facilitates partnerships, strategic alliances, and other ventures that promote social and economic justice. SVN compiles and promotes best practices for socially responsible enterprises and produces unique conferences that support the professional and personal development of business leaders and social entrepreneurs.

Please visit http://www.svn.org for more information on SVN membership, initiatives, and events.

# About the Author

**Mark Albion** is a social entrepreneur who has cofounded seven organizations, including Net Impact, an international network of MBA students and professionals committed to using the power of business to create a better world. He wrote the *New York Times* business bestseller *Making a Life, Making a Living*® based on his twelve-year-old monthly *Making a Life* e-newsletter, which is read in eighty-seven countries. Formerly, Albion was a student and professor at Harvard University and its Business School for eighteen years. He was profiled on *60 Minutes,* praised by leaders as diverse as Ronald Reagan and Mother Teresa, and dubbed "the savior of b-school souls" by *Business-Week* for his efforts to nourish our next generation of business leaders.

Please visit http://www.makingalife.com for more information on Mark's 3,500 word monthly e-newsletter, his audio CDs, and his books and to access his *Fast Company* career columns.

**Values-Driven Business: How to Change the World, Make Money, and Have Fun**
*by Ben Cohen and Mal Warwick*
This short, easy-to-read book details every step in the process of creating and managing a small or midsized business that will reflect your personal values, not force you to hide them. As co-founder of the immensely successful Ben & Jerry's Homemade Ice Cream, Ben Cohen is one of the best-known examples of personal integrity and social commitment in the business community. Social Venture Network chair Mal Warwick is the leader of one of the world's oldest and most respected organizations committed to building a just and sustainable world through business. Using down-to-earth language and abundant examples, they combine their decades of experience to show how virtually any small business can be efficient, competitive, and successful while pursuing a "triple bottom line" of profit, people, and planet.
*February 2006, $12.00, paperback. ISBN 978-1-57675-358-3 or 1-57675-358-1*

**Marketing That Matters: 10 Practices to Drive Your Socially Responsible Business**
*by Chip Conley and Eric Friedenwald-Fishman*
"Marketing" is not a dirty word or a last resort—it is key to advancing the mission of any socially responsible business. In this book, award-winning marketers Chip Conley and Eric Friedenwald-Fishman offer values-driven businesspeople an in-the-trenches guide to building effective marketing models for their companies. For overworked entrepreneurs and socially conscious corporate leaders who want to match their mission with their values but lack the time or the training to develop a

strategy from scratch, this field manual provides practical steps for incorporating marketing as a core element of the business. Full of inspiring stories, key concepts, and tested advice, this book shows how to sell what you do without selling your soul.
*October 2006, $12.00, paperback, ISBN 978-1-57675-383-5 or 1-57675-383-2*

Growing Local Value: How to Build a Values-Driven Business That Strengthens Your Community
*by Laury Hammel and Gun Denhart*
This down-to-earth guide explains how to build or expand a values-driven business that is deeply embedded in the life of the local community. While most people think of "community engagement" only in terms of philanthropy or volunteerism, entrepreneurs Laury Hammel and Gun Denhart show how every aspect of a business (from product creation to employee recruitment to vendor selection to raising capital) holds the dual promise of bigger profits and a stronger local community. Including practical tools such as a Community Involvement Self-Assessment, *Growing Local Value* explores the full spectrum of ways in which a business can contribute to its community—and the benefits it receives when it does.
*November 2006, $12.00, paperback, ISBN 978-1-57675-371-2 or 1-57675-371-9*


**For more information, check out the
Social Venture Network Series Web page:
www.svnbooks.com.**

# About Berrett-Koehler Publishers

**Berrett-Koehler** is an independent publisher dedicated to an ambitious mission: Creating a World That Works for All.

We believe that to truly create a better world, action is needed at all levels—individual, organizational, and societal. At the individual level, our publications help people align their lives with their values and with their aspirations for a better world. At the organizational level, our publications promote progressive leadership and management practices, socially responsible approaches to business, and humane and effective organizations. At the societal level, our publications advance social and economic justice, shared prosperity, sustainability, and new solutions to national and global issues.

A major theme of our publications is "Opening Up New Space." They challenge conventional thinking, introduce new ideas, and foster positive change. Their common quest is changing the underlying beliefs, mind-sets, institutions, and structures that keep generating the same cycles of problems, no matter who our leaders are or what improvement programs we adopt.

We strive to practice what we preach—to operate our publishing company in line with the ideas in our books. At the core of our approach is *stewardship,* which we define as a deep sense of responsibility to administer the company for the benefit of all of our "stakeholder" groups: authors, customers, employees, investors, service providers, and the communities and environment around us.

We are grateful to the thousands of readers, authors, and other friends of the company who consider themselves to be part of the "BK Community." We hope that you, too, will join us in our mission.

# Be Connected

## Visit Our Website

Go to www.bkconnection.com to read exclusive previews and excerpts of new books, find detailed information on all Berrett-Koehler titles and authors, browse subject-area libraries of books, and get special discounts.

## Subscribe to Our Free E-Newsletter

Be the first to hear about new publications, special discount offers, exclusive articles, news about bestsellers, and more! Get on the list for our free e-newsletter by going to www.bkconnection.com.

## Participate in the Discussion

To see what others are saying about our books and post your own thoughts, check out our blogs at www.bkblogs.com.

## Get Quantity Discounts

Berrett-Koehler books are available at quantity discounts for orders of ten or more copies. Please call us toll-free at (800) 929-2929 or email us at bkp.orders@aidcvt.com.

## Host a Reading Group

For tips on how to form and carry on a book reading group in your workplace or community, see our website at www.bkconnection.com.

## Join the BK Community

Thousands of readers of our books have become part of the "BK Community" by participating in events featuring our authors, reviewing draft manuscripts of forthcoming books, spreading the word about their favorite books, and supporting our publishing program in other ways. If you would like to join the BK Community, please contact us at bkcommunity@bkpub.com.